# A BIBLIOGRAPHICAL SURVEY OF ROTATING SAVINGS AND CREDIT ASSOCIATIONS

Alaine Low

Oxfam (UK and Ireland)
Banbury Road, Oxford, OX2 7DZ

Centre for Cross-Cultural Research on Women
Queen Elizabeth House
University of Oxford

© CCCRW 1995

Practical Action Publishing Ltd
25 Albert Street, Rugby, CV21 2SD, Warwickshire, UK
www.practicalactionpublishing.com

First published by Oxfam UK in 1995.
Reprinted by Practical Action Publishing

© Oxfam 1995

Oxfam GB is registered as a charity in England and Wales (no. 202918) and Scotland (SCO 039042).
Oxfam GB is a member of Oxfam International.

Paperback ISBN: 9780855982980
PDF ISBN: 9780855986643

A catalogue record for this publication is available from the British Library.

All rights reserved. Reproduction, copy, transmission, or translation of any part of this publication may be made only under the following conditions:

• with the prior written permission of the publisher; or
• with a licence from the Copyright Licensing Agency Ltd., 90 Tottenham Court Road, London W1P 9HE, UK, or from another national licensing agency; or
• for quotation in a review of the work; or
• under the terms set out below.

This publication is copyright, but may be reproduced by any method without fee for teaching purposes, but not for resale. Formal permission is required for all such uses, but normally will be granted immediately. For copying in any other circumstances, or for re-use in other publications, or for translation or adaptation, prior written permission must be obtained from the publisher, and a fee may be payable.

Designed and typeset by Oxfam Design Department
Oxfam GB is a member of Oxfam International

Reasonable efforts have been made to publish reliable data and information, but the author and publisher cannot assume responsibility for the validity of all materials or for the consequences of their use.

The manufacturer's authorised representative in the EU for product safety is Lightning Source France, 1 Av. Johannes Gutenberg, 78310 Maurepas, France. compliance@lightningsource.fr

# PREFACE

Shirley Ardener and Sandra Burman

Rotating Savings and Credit Associations, in diverse forms, have existed in various locations in this century and probably long before; how long depends on how one defines them. Possibly they derive from forms of co-operation which had roots in a neighbourliness which offered help in kind or in labour in a predictable, regular way. It was only in the early nineteen-sixties that researchers began to notice how widespread ROSCAs were, Clifford Geertz and Shirley Ardener being possibly the first to collect comparative material from different cultural groups. Geertz, who had worked in Java, concerned himself primarily with Asian material. Ardener had first-hand experience of ROSCAs as they operated among a group of rural Ibo in Nigeria, publishing a paper giving detailed case material of their significance and processes in a specific cultural context (Ardener 1953). At that time, for most people in her study, they were the only practicable way of acquiring credit, other than by borrowing from family or a moneylender; banks and aid agencies had made little impact then. They also provided a welcome discipline to saving. When Polly Hill, who worked in Ghana, requested information, Ardener sent her a memorandum on the comparative material which she had collected, which on Hill's advice was augmented and published (1964b). The major problem requiring to be addressed then was the paucity of good published material. The scattered data available was only rarely rich and detailed, and her paper was designed to stimulate new research collected more systematically. Better description seemed urgently needed before any general analyses could be undertaken. Indeed, it was a survey of the literature, not altogether unlike that undertaken thirty years later at our invitation by Alaine Low. It is disappointing that, although more material is now available, Low's plea for more detailed case material for analysis is still all too relevant.

Although some interest in ROSCAs continued, it was in the 1980s, as Low notes below, that researchers increasingly confirmed cases, not of the general demise of ROSCAs which Geertz had forecast, but of their survival and even expansion. New work began to accumulate. The proliferation of aid donors and schemes for developing the economies of Africa and Asia through formal programmes and institutions - and the failure of many of these - drew the comparatively successful ROSCAs, as part of the so-called informal sector of their economies, to the attention of economists, some of whom augmented the literature with useful new material and questions. Nevertheless, the papers by Geertz and Ardener, despite their dates of publication, were still given places in the debates as useful introductions or as points of comparison and departure.

In 1987, at an international symposium attended by Shirley Ardener held at the Africa Studiecentrum in Leiden on the political economy of Cameroon, the importance of ROSCAs, not only to the rural and urban disadvantaged but also to successful Cameroon entrepreneurs, recurred in the discussions. Margaret Niger-Thomas, for example, introduced some interesting ideas about their significance as a budgeting device for women in Mamfe. While these talks were conducted in Leiden, Dr Sandra Burman was working among disadvantaged women in South Africa who impressed upon her the importance they gave to ROSCAs. From these two experiences a plan emerged to hold an international workshop at the Centre for Cross-Cultural Research on Women.

It seemed timely first to put in hand a literature survey which would up-date earlier work. We invited Dr Alaine Low to undertake this task, as she had wide experience in Africa, Cyprus, the Caribbean and Latin America. Trained as an economic historian, she had worked on entrepreneurship and economic diversification in Peru, and had carried out a lengthy study of the role of British Commercial Banks in the Commonwealth, particularly in some of those formerly administered as British colonies. The assignment which Low undertook for the Centre proved no easy task, and one which, though somewhat exhausting, by its nature could not be exhaustive. Oxford is comparatively well-endowed with libraries which, besides countless books, house a wide range of journals. In addition to those tracked down by Dr Low, a number of colleagues, including some contributors to the workshop, kindly provided references to titles, not all of which could be consulted but which have been included in her bibliography for completeness.

Dr Low was not asked to limit her enquiry only to those studies which singled out the role of women in ROSCAs. Indeed, most studies of ROSCAs have been 'gender blind', differences which might have interested us being lost in the aggregations. She has, however, drawn special attention to those works which she could identify as having considered the significance of ROSCAs for women. Her introduction is a working document, a bibliographical exercise which usefully provides leads to guide researchers towards material relevant to their interests; it reflects the distribution, the occasional richness, and the patchiness still of the material currently available. It is hoped that soon the quality of the corpus will be suitably enhanced, and gaps will be filled, as a result of this document and the book associated with it. We would welcome, from readers, potential entries based on published works not covered here, or amendments, so that this survey can be up-dated from time to time.

The Centre's workshop which was held in Oxford in January 1992 brought together African researchers (Dr Ellen Bortei-Doku, Margaret Niger-Thomas, Dr Astier Almedom, Sarah Massengo, Nozipho Lembete) and Africanists (including, as well as ourselves, Sally (E.M.) Chilver and Dr Mike Rowlands). From Bangladesh and India came Dr Hameeda Hossein and Dr Raj Mohini Sethi, while Linda Mayoux spoke about cotton reelers in Pakistan. Shaila Srinivasan offered comparative material on Asian women in Oxford. Dr Otto Hospes embodied his extensive research on ROSCAs in a paper on Indonesia. Dr Joy Hendry talked about the eclipse of ROSCAs in Japan, while Professor Ivan Light described their critical importance to the notably successful entrepreneurs of Korean derivation in the United States of America. Dr Sue Szabo made sure that some consideration was given to various credit institutions in Latin America, although she had no material on ROSCA use there. The Caribbean picture was brought to our attention by Dr Jean Besson while, closer to home, Jane Khatib-Chahidi and Sophia Koufopoulou discussed material from Cyprus and Turkey. All these papers are alluded to in Low's survey below; most of them are to be found in a volume based upon the workshop: *Money-Go-Rounds: The Importance of ROSCAs for Women* (eds S. Ardener and S. Burman, Berg Press, 1995), which also includes papers by Hazel Summerfield on Somali women in London and by Kuniko Miyanaga on Japan.

It remains for us to thank Dr Low for undertaking this survey within severe time constraints. We are indebted to Oxfam for a generous grant towards the cost of preparing it and for their help towards the expenses of the aforementioned volume, published by Berg Press. The Overseas Development Administration, and the British Council, through its offices in London and overseas, kindly met some of the costs of bringing researchers to the workshop; to those contributors who arrived at their own expense special thanks are due.

We hope that readers will find this working document useful and, with Dr Low, we welcome information on studies not included here, of which there must be many, so that it may be up-dated. Implicit is a plea, which echoes that of the comparative survey written by Ardener nearly thirty years ago, for better, more systematic studies of ROSCAs, imbued with a greater appreciation of the general literature. The lack of such awareness may account for the sense of discovery which some researchers still exhibit, and from which perhaps that romanticism which Low detects possibly derives. Yet ROSCAs do seem to be capable of embodying a moral dimension. Good personal relationships between members are often of great concern to them, and not only because reputation is an economic asset. Social solidarity and advancement of the community is usually important both to individuals and as a cultural objective of the group of members, or of the wider community of which they are a part. Indeed, perhaps members sometimes 'sugar' what they see as an unacceptable 'pill' of raw commercialism and personal utility, which may lie at the centre of ROSCA activity, by stressing their sociability and support of the common good. The dependency or asymmetry implicit in credit-taking may be masked by the members placing an emphasis on their savings feature rather than their credit function. It is, perhaps, not surprising that, even in the light of their known limitations, the durability of ROSCAs, the undoubted benefits they can provide for the disadvantaged as well as for the successful entrepreneur, should produce advocates, especially in a world where economic failure is so common.

# A BIBLIOGRAPHICAL SURVEY OF ROTATING SAVINGS AND CREDIT ASSOCIATIONS

Alaine Low

**Definition of ROSCAs**

Ardener provided a definition of ROSCAs, which, following Geertz, she called Rotating Credit Associations (Ardener 1964) and which has been accepted by almost all other scholars (Shanmugan 1991), Chipeta being an exception (Chipeta and Mkandawire 1991). The abbreviation RCA has, however, been largely superseded by that of ROSCA (Rotating Savings and Credit Association), because there is currently an emphasis on the function of such associations in the mobilization of savings. Adams and Ghate have suggested reasons for the early emphasis on loans, and credit rather than savings (Adams and Ghate 1992). It is clear however, from much of the research, that for the participants, saving is their predominant interest, not credit. There is evidence for this from many communities; for example, in Bolivia 91% of those involved said saving was their main motive (Adams 1984).

When Ardener wrote her article, which was a review of the literature and a listing of the geographical spread of the associations, she found 62 published references to associations that met the criteria she established for rotating credit associations. Since the mid-1960s there has been a growth in the academic studies of ROSCAs, with some useful, but partial, literature listings (Hospes 1992a & b; Kerri 1976; Miracle et al 1980). There has been a marked increase in the number of publications per annum since about 1985. The accompanying listing of works on or relevant to a study of ROSCAs cannot claim to be exhaustive. It is largely confined to works in the English language, although there are references to French, German, Dutch and Japanese writings. Relatively little has been written by scholars in the developing world where these associations flourish, with the exception of the Nigerians (and to a lesser extent the Ghanaians) (Adeyemo 1983; Ezeabasili 1960; Ijere 1963; Isong 1959; Mbat 1985; Nafziger 1977; Ngozi 1982; Nwabughuogu 1984; Okonjo 1979; Osuntogun 1981).

The two areas best researched are probably West Africa and Indonesia, but there is also a substantial body of relevant writing for Ethiopia, India and South Africa. There appears to be little on the Middle East and North Africa, and in Japan ROSCAs seem to be dying out. Although the existence of ROSCAs is documented for Latin America (Peru, Bolivia, Mexico, Guatemala, Brazil) there appear to be few studies, in spite of the great interest of academics in the informal economic sector. A breakdown of citations by geographical area follows the main alphabetical listing of articles and books.

**Overview of the literature on ROSCAs**

Much of the large body of academic writing on the associations is descriptive and in the form of case studies. These permit the identification of general characteristics of the associations, but do not give much indication of their importance to the economy as a whole (Adams and Ghate 1992; Wu 1974). The literature provides a fairly comprehensive view of the geographical spread of the associations and makes it clear that one can expect to find them in 'developing' and 'developed' countries alike, although there seems to be a preponderance of them in the former.

Beyond the descriptive level the literature is often disappointing in that it is not problem-oriented. The literature reviewed for this paper is drawn, in the main, from specialist journal articles and one would expect some focus. This is not always the case. It would seem that, apart from a few notable exceptions, those writing on the subject are not well-read in the existing literature, and in some cases are ignorant of the existence of ROSCAs in other countries (see for example Wainaina 1989). The host of micro-studies, besides giving a good idea of their location, usually documents the procedures followed by various forms of ROSCAs, but often little else. The main problem is lack of methodology.

There have been two main categories of contributors to the literature: those interested in rural credit and anthropologists who, while researching some other issue, have gathered information and written up their material on ROSCAs but who have made relatively little sustained or systematic study of them. Bouman noted this in 1977 and called for quantitative research. More recently he reiterated this plea in 1990.

ROSCAs are said to have a role in building social capital. Social capital is of particular interest for the study of women and ROSCAs. Although the collection of essays edited by Firth and Yamey (1964) includes some comment on social capital, one would certainly expect much more from anthropologists on this, given its important impact on development. More recently, social capital has been explored by political scientists and historians (Coleman 1990), there is little treatment of it in the literature on ROSCAs (Kerri 1976).

One school of thought views ROSCAs as a response to deprivation. This is discussed by Wu (1974), but not taken up by many authors. Those economists especially interested in rural credit do have an analytical approach to ROSCAs, but they give relatively little recognition to the work of anthropologists. Few writers have dealt with the issues raised by Geertz (1962), who suggested that ROSCAs formed a 'middle rung' in economic development and that they would die out as economies became more sophisticated (but see Hospes 1992a; Kurtz 1973; Newark 1990; Wu 1974); see also Hamer (1981) for a discussion of the importance of ROSCAs in transitional periods in society, and the recent study by Nelson (1995). Ardener produced a schedule for field research in 1964 (Ardener 1964), but by the 1970s some saw her work as too concerned with the organizational side of ROSCAs (Kerri 1976; Wu 1974). There is little in the literature on the risk issue, not enough on mechanisms to deal with inflation, and very little perspective on how important ROSCAs are in terms of national development.

There is perhaps a danger of romanticizing ROSCAs. Relatively few articles deal with the limitations of the clubs (Haggblade 1978; Hamer 1981; Rowlands 1995). There is some evidence of corruption, for example in Nigeria, Uganda and India (Bascom 1952; Hamer 1981; Nelson 1995; Sethi 1995) and strong-arm tactics to force possible defaulters to pay up are noted (Bortei-Dorku and Aryeetey 1995), but much more research is needed in this area. Further work is also needed on alternative sources of credit, although recently there has been more in this area by economists. There is, for example, important work by Bouman and others on pawnbrokers (Bouman and Houtman 1988). Evidence on the preferences of savers and borrowers within the informal sector is found in the literature but this is not highly developed.

It is difficult to obtain an historical perspective from the literature. There are only a few articles which deal with this (Nwabughuogu 1984; Izumida 1992). An interesting angle would be the changing attitudes of government (and of aid organizations) to such associations (Ardener 1964). There has been overt hostility to ROSCAs in a number of countries (Bouman 1977; Knez n.d.; Adeyeye 1970; Fernando 1986). Ardener cites Hill who noted that ROSCAs were considered 'a social evil' in Ghana in the 1960s. In South Africa there has been police harassment (Lukhele 1990). Is there a notable change in approach because other development and small credit schemes have achieved little? Few of the papers look at the legal framework in which ROSCAs operate, although Sethi's chapter is an exception (Sethi 1995). Although regulated in some countries (e.g. India), in others this is not the case (Chipeta and Mkandawire 1992). Could federations of ROSCAs act as pressure groups for change? There was some evidence for this in Nigeria, and a recent federation of associations in South Africa has ambitions of forging itself into a powerful pressure group (Lukhele 1990; Burman and Lembete 1995).

## Terminology

Terminology obviously varies between countries. Local names of associations can be found in most case studies and are listed in some surveys (Ardener 1964; Bouman 1977; Due and Summary 1982; Jerome 1991; Miracle et al 1980). A list of names given to the associations is attached. The names invariably signify some sort of community activity or derive from the name of the money fund, e.g. *box-money, boxi*. The participants are often referred to as 'players', sometimes as 'throwers' (Besson 1995), and the contributions may be termed the 'hand' or 'shares'. Sometimes the association may be known by the name of the purpose to which the share-outs are to be put, e.g. 'kitchen ROSCAs' (Niger-Thomas 1995), or named after the day on which members meet. Ardener restricts the terminology used for the funds to 'pool' or 'take-out', but some authors use other terminology which is also self-explanatory.

## Characteristics of the schemes

Ardener's definition of a ROSCA (Ardener 1964) gives the essential characteristics, stressing the importance of the rotating element, but beyond this there is immense variation. The schemes vary considerably from country to country and from group to group. However, using Ardener's definition as a starting point, certain characteristics are common to all. The associations are flexible, accessible, and designed to meet users' needs. Arrangements for pay-outs vary and include drawing lots for first turn, by bidding, and by the decision of the chairperson. Sometimes bribes are involved (Niger-Thomas 1995). In some set-ups it is possible to alter the order of the rotation on compassionate grounds (Bouman 1990). ROSCAs are valued as a means of enforced savings (Fernando 1986; Nelson 1995). Economists (e.g. von Pischke 1991) stress the low transaction costs. Mutual trust is an essential characteristic, indeed 'reputation' holds the place that collateral does in the formal sector (Szabo 1992). Another critical characteristic of the classic association is the clear-cut end of cycle which is reached when each participant has received his/her pay-out. The cycle may then start again with some or all of the same members, or may be wound up. Thus each member knows at the outset how long the commitment lasts. The length of a ROSCA's cycle may vary; for example, the rotation may last for only one day (Nayar 1973), it may continue for ten days, or it may take as long as two or three years before each member has received their take-out. There is even mention of 20 years in Nepal in the 1960s (Seibel and Shrestha 1988).

## Geographical spread

Rotating credit associations may be found on four continents: Africa, Asia, the Americas and Europe; although I found no record possibly Australia may be included. In Africa the west is best documented, particularly Cameroon, Nigeria and Ghana. They are widespread in Asia. In India until relatively recently the schemes were concentrated in the south; 33% of India's *chit* funds were in Kerela state (Nayar 1986). In the United States of America they are found among recent immigrant communities, and they are documented in Central and South America. Forms of ROSCAs are known in Europe among indigenous people and minority ethnic groups. Studies of the United Kingdom include Sethi (1995) and Srinivasan (1995), Summerfield (1995), Tebbut (1983).

Migration, forced and voluntary, has led to the systems being introduced into new areas, and the same or 'corrupt' forms of the original names are often in use (Besson forthcoming). In some areas, like Mauritius, there are ROSCAs based on two separate models (Benedict 1964). The possibility of the transfer of the idea from Africa by slaves to the Americas was suggested in 1964 by Ardener, who noted that, while they are found in the Caribbean, Afro-Americans in the United States of America did not form them, although there is some evidence that they are joining now (Crowley 1953). It is unclear to what extent this has been researched since. In Malaya ROSCAs may have been introduced from India (Shanmugar 1991). Many of the associations have a long history, pre-dating a monetized economy, and some seem to have originated, as in Southern India, as grain stores. More recently, as in Uganda, they appear to have grown out of drinking clubs (Heald 1986). There seems to be a close association with brewing, drinking and women's associations in several parts of Africa, particularly in the south and east. Similar links are not apparent in Latin America or Asia.

In some parts of the world ROSCAs are increasing in number and popularity. This confounds the argument of Geertz (1962), who thought that they would die out as economies became more sophisticated and monetarized. In 1979 Bouman thought it possible that they had died out in Vietnam (Bouman 1979), and it seems that they are disappearing in Japan (Hendry 1992). In South Korea, however, they are flourishing. They became more widespread in Malaysia between 1975 and 1989 (Shanmugan 1989). One must assume that they meet a need that the formal sector is failing at present. Some commentators on West Africa suggest that ROSCAs may become increasingly important as commercial banks retreat from the rural areas. ROSCAs co-exist with formal banking organizations, not only in developing countries, but also in developed countries such as the United States of America. In South Africa virtually all the women members of the urban associations studies by Burman and Lembete (1995) held bank accounts. In India one-third of *chit* funds are in Kerela state (Nayar 1986; Nayar 1992), one-quarter are in Tamil Nadu, while Andhra Pradesh and Karnathka come third and fourth in importance with regard to ROSCAs. In the southern states there is also greater banking density than elsewhere and literacy rates are high compared with other states.

## Membership of ROSCAs

The associations are used by all socio-economic classes (Anderson 1966). However, membership of any individual ROSCA tends to be homogeneous. Increasingly, members may hold bank accounts. In some countries bank employees belong to ROSCAs (Ardener 1964), and there is evidence that IMF officials have their own scheme (Adams 1992). Employees of Oxfam in Tanzania operate their own ROSCA (Massengo 1992). It would be a mistake, therefore, to view the associations as catering exclusively for the poor. Membership in some cases is valued for the social contact which may be involved (Bouman 1979; Burman and Lembete 1995; Khatib-Chahidi 1995; Koufopoulou 1992). There is relatively little in the literature about the secondary functions of ROSCAs in cementing friendships. Traditional social functions of the associations are reported to be strong in some areas (Begashaw 1978; Bouman and Harteveld 1976; Bouman and Moll 1992; Gedamu 1972), while in others, largely in Asia (Bouman 1984), but also in Nigeria, they are reported to be declining in importance. Here the financial aspects of the clubs predominate. The size of a ROSCA group is usually, but not invariably, small, but there is immense variation; in New Guinea, for example, among the Hageners as small as two (Strathern 1975); as many as 100 in Sanghi, India (Bouman 1989), and larger elsewhere.

## The advantages of ROSCAs

The advantages of ROSCAs are the same as those of many other schemes in the informal sector: they are accessible and local, and do not involve travel to a banking centre which is often in a town (von Pischke 1992). Transaction costs are kept to a minimum; bureaucratic procedures are, in the main, absent, and there is a general appreciation of the 'secrecy' of such organizations. Aryeetey and Gockel provide detailed data on why market women tend not to save with banks (Aryeetey and Gockel 1991). Many fear that banks and institutions in the formal sector may make financial information available to government authorities, and certainly in some countries ROSCA money is considered to be 'black money' (Light and Bonachiche 1988).

Membership does not normally involve collateral, though it is clear that there are situations where participants are drawn from socio-economic classes where most, if not all, are substantial property owners and/or hold bank accounts. Payments are usually in cash but may be in kind (Bouman 1977). Saving may take various forms, for example the purchase of gold coins (Khatib-Chahidi 1995; Koufopoulou 1992). Wage earners may operate a scheme for regular deductions from their pay. Membership may be restricted or unrestricted, for example to the compound members in the case of the Yoruba women (Bascom 1952).

### Age and adaptability of ROSCAs

Some ROSCAs predate monetization, and originally, if not currently, dealt in grain or livestock. In southern India today women may save handfuls of rice (Mayoux 1995). The associations are very adaptable. Where they used to cater for traditional needs (e.g. weddings, funerals, and other ritualistic ceremonies) they now cater for education, house construction, taxes, fertilizer funds, working capital or travel funds (Hendry 1992; Massengo 1992; Srinivasan 1995; Summerfield 1995). Different systems of allocation have evolved to meet changing times and credit needs. Some still reflect seasonal needs related to harvesting, vacation times, and so on. Arrangements, in general, seem to have become more complex in India than in Africa (Nayar 1973).

### Procedures

Procedures can be very simple or very complex. Much of the literature devotes a good deal of space to describing procedural matters. These may involve a simple distribution at each meeting, may be complicated systems to allow some recompense for the chair-person, and/or some interest for those who pick up their take-out last, and so on. Some work according to a predetermined list of who gets the first take-out, others have a lottery, some auction the right. Hospes discusses how this varies according to the primary function of the *arisan* - those with a social purpose pay out frequently, using a lottery system; those with an economic purpose have a lottery and reach a consensus about need (Hospes 1992a). Some savers in Trinidad (Levin 1975) prefer to take their turn last. Distribution by lottery provides a gambling element which has a strong appeal in some societies. There is a full discussion of the procedures in Ardener (1964).

Discipline is essential (von Pischke 1992). Most critics stress the point that default rates are better than those of commercial banks and other institutions in the formal sector (Adams and Ladman 1979; Christen 1992; Cope and Kurtz 1979), partly because of careful selection of members, but also because of the disgrace which falls upon backsliders. In some areas 'strong-arm' tactics make people pay. Where there are potential defaulters, risks are often reduced by placing them last in the rotation cycle, as in Sri Lanka (Bouman 1984). Fernando (1986), writing on Sri Lanka, discusses the sanction of ostracism. The poor may be very well motivated to repay because of their desperate need for further access to loans (Biggs and others 1991).

### Can ROSCAs cope with inflation and interest payments?

Bouman (1990) writes of misunderstandings about the informal financial sector. Clearly there are ways in which ROSCAs cope with inflation. There are cases in India where payment in kind is made (Nayar 1973). Closely related to the inflation issue is that of interest, and many schemes do operate an interest system, although, as noted, the prime concern of the saver may not be interest, but security. Nevertheless, some societies have very complex arrangements which probably cater for inflation. If cycles are short, then the last member to take the kitty may not be greatly disadvantaged. An article by Benedict (1964) on Mauritius shows that while the Indian communities could get around the problem of inflation by making the last first in any new cycle, the Chinese community had an interest-rate system. As noted above, in the Mediterranean area gold coins are used as a hedge against inflation (Khatib-Chahidi 1995; Koufopoulou 1992). ROSCA participants may deposit sums in a bank (for example, in Mali).

This is probably not uncommon but not well documented, but Burman and Lembete (1995) describe the involvement of banks and building societies in South Africa. There is more detail about the type of organizers of ROSCAs and their general business activities.

The relationship between banks and ROSCAs varies greatly with area, social class, and the accessibility of banks. On the one hand ROSCAs may cater for a client in whom the banks have little interest. On the other there may be a good deal of co-operation between the banks and ROSCAs; thus ROSCAs may place money in deposit accounts at a bank. In Ghana, Aryeetey found, the fund, once it had reached a certain magnitude, was used for a down payment at a bank to acquire a loan (Aryeetey 1990). In Asia this practice has probably reached its highest point. In Korea there was fierce competition between ROSCAs and commercial banks, with the latter copying some of the practices of the former (Light and Bonachiche 1988). V. deLancy reports accusations in the Cameroon that ROSCAs, which yield interest for creditors, had become so popular that they had contributed to a liquidity crisis in the banking system (deLancey 1978).

**The popularity of ROSCAs**

The popularity of ROSCAs may be due, in part, to secrecy. The informal nature of the institutions is described by von Pischke as 'the economy beyond the frontier, essentially private' (von Pischke 1991). Their popularity has also been put down to the fear that money held in Post Office savings accounts could be known to tax inspectors (Ardener 1964). Light finds that in the United States of America the Korean immigrant community values the associations in part because some pay illegally high interest rates, and they provide a way of tax evasion (Light and Bonachiche 1988). They are popular with all strata of society in India (Anderson 1966) and Sri Lanka (Bouman 1984), but are more popular with Indians and Malays than the more affluent Chinese in Malaysia (Shanmugan 1989). Payment of relatively low interest rates, though this is not always the case (Isong 1959, Light and Bonachiche 1988), may not be a deterrent to potential members. ROSCAs may act as money markets in a limited way (Ardener 1964). Some members, having picked up the fund, use it to lend to others who belong to the same circle. This practice may be on the increase, especially in Asia.

ROSCAs may be popular because of a feature noted by Ardener: the form of insurance offered by the associations. Members may be happy to forego interest in the knowledge that they have access to funds if there is a crisis and, as noted above, some ROSCAs operate a system of allocation whereby compassionate grounds are taken into consideration. Other associated benefits are the social and economic functions or activities associated with the group, which sometimes include a separate savings fund for a special purpose such as school fees, or (Hospes 1995; Niger-Thomas 1995) welfare or charitable group activity. There are also cases of the establishment of a co-operative store. Another interesting development is that of parallel savings funds for emergency needs. This is not uncommon and may be established as a spontaneous response to a crisis (Ardener 1964).

In Benin, where the ROSCAs are called *Associations Rotatives d'Epargne et de Credit* (AREC), the principal function of the ROSCAs for small traders are acting as 'money-guards' for clients. Money guards are found in other parts of West Africa (Bortei-Dorku and Aryeetey 1995; Katzin 1964; Lelart 1989).

A further benefit of the ROSCA is the enhancement of status afforded by membership of some associations. The importance of auxiliary, non-financial services of the meetings is discussed in relation to a number of countries. These may be informal, as in Ethiopia (Almedom 1991; Gabianu n.d.). Elsewhere, governments or NGOs have introduced other services at ROSCA meetings (e.g. family planning in Indonesia, see Bouman and Moll 1992). Hospes et al (1988) describes the functions of the female government employees' group health care and family planning. Meetings may be social and festive occasions. In certain cases much of the take-out may be spent on entertainment (Ardener 1964, Geertz 1962, Bouman 1990). This was true of

Cameroon in 1976 (Bouman and Harteveld, 1988) but less true of Nigeria at approximately the same time (Bouman 1979). The same could be said of the *arisan* in Indonesia. These social functions seem especially important for migrants to urban areas (Strathern 1975) and to other countries. Although scholars assume there are various auxiliary services at the meetings, some produce relatively little evidence of this. Social functions are dying out in some areas, including Sri Lanka where ROSCAs have become impersonal (Bouman 1984). Shanmugan (1989) reports conflicting evidence on this issue for India. In Ghana today the social functions are more important in the richer urban associations than in the poorer clubs in rural areas (Bortei-Doku 1995). It is possible that the social aspects of ROSCAs are particularly important to women, especially in those areas where they get little opportunity for social contact outside the family circle (Almedom 1995; Koufopoulou 1992; Sethi 1995).

There is tremendous variation among ROSCAs in other respects. For example socio-religious functions seem to be dying out in Nigeria and Japan (Hendry 1992), but remain important in Indonesia (Hospes 1992a).

**Women and rotating credit**

There are few articles that deal specifically with women's associations, approximately 45 were found, although in some countries (e.g. Bolivia) women are 60% of the 'players'(Adams and Canavesi de Sahonero 1988). Among articles dealing specifically with women and rotating credit the following are notable contributions: Bouman 1984; Hospes 1992a; Keirn 1970; Koufopoulou 1992; Lewis 1976; Little 1973; Madge 1991; Ross 1990; Wainaina 1989 and the case studies by Almedon, Besson, Burman and Lembete, Bortei-Doku and Aryeetey, Hospes, Khatib-Chahidi, Light and Deng, Mayoux and Anand Miyanaga, Nelson, Niger-Thomas, Rowlands, Sethi, Srinivasan, and Summerfield in Ardener and Burman 1995). There is material on women for a number of African countries, also for Indonesia, Cyprus, Turkey, India, and immigrant groups in the United Kingdom (Srinivanan 1995). There is considerable and growing literature on access to credit by poor people and discussion about whether access is gender-specific. Women certainly have a poor record of obtaining credit from the formal sector, including access to government schemes, and it would seem that in some countries, at least, they make very few applications for loans (Ahooja-Patel 1990; Berger 1989; Buvinic and Berger 1990; Buvinic and Zeidenstein 1979; Pastizzi-Ferencic et al 1990). The cultural, economic, legal and educational reasons for this have been documented (Lycette 1984). Mendez compares the legal constraints in a large number of countries (Mendez 1990). Technical issues, such as the extent to which the debts incurred by poor people are likely to be repaid, have been addressed by economists. It would seem that the poor are not a high risk group in the informal sector, and particularly within the ROSCA framework, and this is especially the case with women. The poor, in general, often have a very good repayment record because of peer pressure and because of the desire to borrow again. ROSCAs may inculcate good habits. Children are in some cases introduced to saving through ROSCAs (Bouman 1977; Begashaw 1978).

The economic crisis of the 1980s affected female-headed households most adversely, not least in Latin America. Women have been largely ignored in government integrated rural development programmes. The 1970s income-generation schemes for women ran into problems. Many schemes had low income potential or assumed skills which the women did not have. A 1984 study of the Ecuadorian Development Fund (FED) PRODEM project for small business in Quito which is oriented towards women, showed that women used loans differently from male borrowers: to increase efficiency, and to maintain production rather than to expand (Berger 1989; Gomez 1990). One assumes that ROSCAs meet the same financial need. Although the literature suggests that ROSCA money is sometimes used for start-up capital, working capital or social investment, it does not consider these issues in detail.

**Call for further research**

The call for serious and statistical research which was made by Ardener in 1964 was recently renewed by Bouman (1990). There is a paucity of studies on the informal financial markets. This is odd, given the interest in other areas of the informal economy, such as trade, industry, housing, and the services sector. There is, understandably, a lack of statistical data for most areas. Where figures are available for the informal sector, as a whole the sums are surprisingly large. The size of the informal urban credit market in India has been estimated to be at least 20% of that of the formal sector, according to Timberg and Alyar (1984). There is little scientific data on the number of individuals who belong to groups and some people will belong to several schemes simultaneously. Bouman gives an overview of the literature on this for the period 1964-1977 (Bouman 1977). Questions may be posed concerning the incidence of ROSCAs in urban and rural areas, of exclusively female clubs, and of mixed societies. In Indonesia, Hospes, writing on Tulehu, found the majority of groups were female ones (Hospes 1992b). The role women play depends upon the economic and social context. Some societies, where women are the members, are organized by men. Others seem to be managed entirely by women (Nguyen 1949) and in yet others husbands provide the contribution money for women members (Almedom 1995). Some women act on behalf of their husbands (Light and Deng 1995). In a number of societies women like to 'hide' their funds from their menfolk and family members who make demands upon them (Niger-Thomas 1995).

**Methodology**

Hospes has recently provided a good overview of the strengths and weaknesses of the literature, including the classic studies by Ardener and Geertz (Hospes 1992b). There is still some truth in the suggestion made in the 1960s (quoted in Ardener 1964) that the contributions made by anthropologists to an understanding of economic institutions has not been very impressive. In 1977 Bouman commented that relatively little work had been done in terms of analysing the production, consumption and investment preferences of ROSCA participants. There has been further comment on the weakness of the methodology used. Ardener in 1964 provided a questionnaire for field workers, but it focuses on the historical and organizational aspects of ROSCAs, not the uses to which the funds are put. Both Kerri (1976) and Wu (1974) regretted that the work of academics dealing with ROSCAs had not been problem-orientated.

The emphasis on savings and the capacity of even the very poor to save has been overlooked, and was not generally recognized until comparatively recently. Development economists have paid relatively little attention to savings, and the mechanisms for mobilizing savings. It has been left to the monetarists to look at these issues. Bouman in all his work insists on the importance of ROSCAs as savings mechanisms as well as lending institutions. Agricultural economists with their interest in rural credit have shown considerable interest in ROSCAs. It would be helpful to have more research on their role in the transition from agriculture to trading, as suggested by Ardener but challenged elsewhere (Ardener 1964). There may well be a fruitful area of research concerning ROSCAs and the activities of ethnic minority entrepreneurs (Light 1972; Light and Bonachiche 1988; Niger-Thomas 1995; Rowlands 1995). Hamer (1981) sees the ROSCA as playing an important transitional role and easing strains in the political economy of former colonial states. Another area of interest is the role of ROSCAs in enabling investment in human capital, including that through education. This is mentioned in several studies but few give quantitive data (Bortei-Doku and Aryeetey 1995; deLancey 1978; Okonjo 1979). Even on a theme like remittances from urban to rural areas there is little data.

An area covered inadequately in the literature is the legal framework in which ROSCAs operate. In some countries the associations are actually illegal. They are forbidden in Malaysia under the Kootu Funds (Prohibition) Act 1971, and they are regarded with suspicion in Sri Lanka, where the government has tried to control them (Bouman 1984; Shanmugan 1989). In India they are regulated (Nayar 1986; Sethi 1995). The role of the associations in promoting political participation, which would be of considerable interest to both academics and some aid agencies, is hardly mentioned in the literature; Nwabughuogu (1984) is an exception here.

## The importance of ROSCAs

Understanding of savings behaviour, and decisions as to when to defer consumption in order to save, need to be studied at the micro-level. ROSCAs are self-selected micro-units. In 1977 Bouman commented that relatively little work had been done in terms of analysing the production, consumption, and investment preferences of ROSCA participants (Bouman 1977). Some studies show that the poorest saved more relative to their income than the richer members of ROSCAs, as was the case in Sri Lanka (Bouman 1984).

Some of the literature deals with the range of financial institutions, or lack of them, open to those in the informal sector. One might note the ethno-centric bias in the concentration of research on lending institutions and the assumption, until comparatively recently, that the very poor do not save. The poor are keen savers and will pay for the privilege of having someone look after their money. The alternative may be to opt for relative illiquidity by investing in such wealth as property or jewellery. Membership of a ROSCA helps to provide the discipline to save, and there is evidence that it is valued for that purpose. The literature on village moneylenders has until recently been hostile and biased, and written by Westerners (Adams and et al 1984). As indicated above, there is a tendency in some of the literature to present an idealized picture of ROSCAs. However, as we saw, some have been described as exploitative because of very high interest payments. Interestingly enough, most of the research on ROSCAs and the informal sector provides very little evidence that the borrowers in the informal sector complain greatly about interest rates. Participants are much more concerned with access to credit than interest rates. (There is, however, material on Nigeria which states that there was much corruption and complaint.)

ROSCAs may also provide a means of upward social mobility. They may introduce members to new ideas but they may also preserve traditional values and customs (Burman and Lembete 1995; Gedamu 1972; Koufopoulou 1992). They may provide a way to express ethnic solidarity.

The relationship between kin and ROSCAs is complex. Ardener summarizes research in the area up to 1964. In some societies membership of the groups is almost an extension of kinship obligations, in others close male kin are forbidden to belong to the same groups as it might prove a cause of friction and stress (Bascom 1952).

## Development issues

Geertz (1964) wrote of ROSCAs as the 'middle rung' in economic development, assuming that there would be a progression to banks and other institutions in the formal sector. The All-Indian Rural Credit Survey recommended that ROSCAs be incorporated into co-operatives. To some extent this was done in Sierre Leone (Ardener 1964). Some writers note that the success of co-operatives owes something to the pre-existence of ROSCAs (Osuntogun and Adeyemo 1981), while others see the latter as transforming themselves into a different type of loan and savings organization (deLancey 1977; Lamberte 1992). The position varies from region to region and there is disagreement among writers over these issues (Illy 1978).

There is much to be said for mobilizing savings which stay within the area and are not syphoned off by the formal banking system to the credit-worthy of the urban areas. This issue is pertinent to the search for ways of incorporating the informal sector, and especially savings groups, into the formal sector, or at least strengthening ties with banks and government agencies. It is an area of interest to NGOs and aid agencies. Bouman, writing on Sri Lanka, noted that the ROSCAs have undergone a major face-lift. Organizers are now usually business people with a solid financial reputation. They like to take the management role because it enhances their reputation, creates goodwill, and gives them access to working capital, as they are usually entitled to the first draw on the fund (Bouman 1984). Experienced business people gain access to ROSCA funds for short-term capital needs, or use the cash for money lending.

In these respects the ROSCAs are already well integrated into the rural and/or urban informal money markets.

The literature documents few examples where ROSCAs have been incorporated into other schemes, although South African developments provide some interesting possibilities (Burman and Lembete 1995). There are, however, examples of successful saving and/or loan schemes which may owe something to the ROSCA model, if indirectly. 'Lessons learned' have been incorporated in the Grameen Bank, Bangladesh, and the Badan Kredit Kecamatan Indonesia Java (Biggs et al 1991). There is some discussion in the general literature of the lessons in relation to Latin America and elsewhere (Seibel and Parhusip 1992). Much of the literature on rural credit for developing countries looks at the reasons for the failure of cheap credit schemes and considers the value of closer links or full integration between the formal and informal financial sectors. Germidis (1990) discusses policy attitudes and recommendations relating to linkage or integration of the two sectors. Mechanism for keeping the savings in rural areas and not draining them off to towns is discussed in Fischer (1988). The issue of whether ROSCAs should be integrated with other financial institutions was discussed in the 1970s (Bouman 1977). Chandavarkar (1985) comments on ways to strengthen links. It should be noted that participation in a ROSCA can increase one's credit rating with financial institutions in the formal sector in some countries. It seems that it is in Asia that the links between the formal and informal sectors are closest. A recent study by Holt and Ribe (1991) makes strong recommendations for caution to those contemplating any type of intervention in ROSCAs.

**The impact of international financial trends on ROSCAs.**

Interest in ROSCAs may well have grown with the increase in the costs of credit. The problems of lending small sums to the landless are several. Transaction costs are high, management effort is great, and borrowers are very vulnerable to economic shocks of whatever origin (Biggs and others 1991). Bouman writes that these concerns influence financial agencies, but do they actually influence those who form the associations? It is not easy to obtain evidence of the growth in the numbers of ROSCAs in general. In some areas the associations have grown fast in the last decade, filling a gap in the financial structures, and (in Korea and Cameroon) rivalling banks, but, as noted above, in other areas on the same continent they may be in decline (Hendry 1981; Izumida 1992; Light and Bonachiche 1988). The evidence is that they evolve to meet new needs rather than that they die out.

**ROSCAs as a means of capital formation**

There is some treatment in the literature of this theme (Chilke 1983; Mbat 1985), but in general there is much descriptive material and not much analysis. There is not a great deal of information on how much is saved, although Chilke (1983), Mbat (1985), Bouman and others quote large sums, even for stagnant economies like Ethiopia. There are discussions about the use of the funds: whether they are assigned to consumption or investment. It is doubtful if these are useful or valid distinctions when we are often dealing with household units of production and consumption. In Nigeria ROSCA funds are more important for start-up capital than working capital, but in each case loans from family and friends were more significant and popular (Adeyemo 1983).

There is no evidence that the smaller, less rich, associations are less rational than those patronized by the wealthy, but emphasis may be placed on different functions (Ardener 1964). There is some evidence that the use to which funds are put are determined by the age of the participants. Little appears to go into productive investment in agriculture and perhaps that is why economists have not been very interested in them. However, deLancy (1988) notes that in Cameroon (c.1983) very few loans from any source were taken out for farming. She found the greatest number of loans from the ROSCAs were for consumption. This was in contrast to those of the credit unions. This is a very complex area, however, because of the fungibility of loans. It is difficult to trace the full value of the funds to a particular project. ROSCAs are probably not used for agriculture because the returns on agriculture are slow and often not substantial. Evidence from West Africa suggests that most of the ROSCA funds go on consumption, education, and taxes (Harteveld 1972).

There is not much discussion on the limitations on the scope and importance of ROSCAs, although the work of Rowlands on Cameroon suggests that ROSCAs may lead to short-term business strategies (Rowlands 1995). This may indicate other structural constraints in the country. A number of authors see little role for ROSCAs in significant economic development (Kurtz and Showman 1978).

**Lessons to be learned**

Konig and Koch (1990), Holt and Ribe (1991), Ladman and Afecha (1990), examine the growth constraints on small enterprises in less developed countries. One study (Konig and Koch 1990) reviews the Colombian government's National Plan for the Development of the Micro-Enterprise and the role of the banks under the scheme. It recommends ten innovations, several of which are similar to the advantages of the ROSCAs. Dupuy (1990) looks at the adaptability of the informal sector, contrasting it to the state's failure in West Africa. He sees the dynamism of the village associations as being a result of state failure. Padmanabhan (1988), in a section on linking informal savings clubs with other financial institutions, provides some material on Ethiopia, where the *ikub* is extremely popular and membership is said to have included 60% of the population in the period 1968-73, while 8-10% of GDP was estimated to have been saved through *ikubs*. He writes that there is evidence that a set of government policies in Taiwan, which included pricing, marketing, land tenure, technology, and public investment, gave a strong impetus to saving for on-farm investment. Some studies do point to lessons to be learned from ROSCAs, particularly in the area of rural credit and savings mobilization. Writers are divided about the advisability of 'interventions', and on balance those with more detailed understanding of the associations advise caution in trying to alter ROSCAs or integrate them into the formal sector (Szabo 1992). Seibel and Shrestha (1988) provide some comments from ROSCA participants in Nepal on the value of links with banks. It is crucial to understand the risk factor, which has received little treatment. Any intervention is likely to disadvantage those which it seeks to benefit, and the ROSCAs themselves may lose credibility.

**WORKS CITED**

Adams, D. W., 'Taking a Fresh Look at Informal Finance', *Informal Finance in Low-Income Countries*, eds Dale W. Adams and D. A. Fitchett, 5-23, Boulder, Westview Press, 1992

----, and Canavesi de Sahonero, Marie L, 'Rotating Savings and Credit Associations in Bolivia', *Savings and Development*, 13, (3), 1988, 219-235

----, and Ghate, P.B., 'Where to from Here in Informal Finance?', *Informal Finance in Low-Income Countries*, eds Dale W. Adams and D. A. Fitchett, 349-359, Boulder, Westview Press, 1992

----, G., Douglas, H., and Von Pischke, J.D., *Undermining Rural Development with Cheap Credit*, Boulder, Colorado, Westview Special Studies in Social, Political, and Economic Development, 1984

----, and Ladman, J. R., 'Lending to the Rural Poor through Informal Groups. A Promising Financial Market Innovation?', *Savings and Development*, 3, (2), 1979, 85-92

Adeyemo, R., 'Credit as an Input in Marketing: a Study of the Nature and Use of Credit by Food Marketeers in Anambra State of Nigeria', *Savings and Development*, 7, (1), 1983, 63-73

Adeyeye, O., 'Cooperative Development through Adaptation: The Nigerian Experience', *Cooperative Information*, 2, 1970

Ahooja-Patel, K., 'Women's Inaccessibility to Credit: Problems and Policies', *Women and Credit*, 6-19, Santo Domingo: United Nations International Research and Training Institute for the Advancement of Women, 1990

Almedom, A. M., 'Aspects of the Growth and Health of the Suckling and Weaning Infant in Ethiopia', D. Phil., Oxford, 1991

----, 'A Note on ROSCAs among Ethiopian Women in Addis Ababa and among Eritrean Women in Oxford', *Money-Go-Rounds: The Importance of ROSCAs for Women*, eds Shirley Ardener and Sandra Burman, Oxford, and Washington, USA, Berg Publishers, 1995

Amogu, O. O. 'Some Notes on Savings in an African Economy', *Social and Economic Studies*, 5, (2), 1956, 202-209

Anderson, R. T., 'Rotating Credit Associations in India', *Economic Development and Cultural Change*, 14, (3), 1966, 334-339

Ardener, S., 'The Comparative Study of Rotating Credit Associations', *The Journal of the Royal Anthropological Institute*, 94, (Part 2), 1964, 201-228; reprinted in Ardener and Burman, 1995

Aryeetey, E., and Gockel, F., *Mobilizing Domestic Resources for Capital Formation in Ghana* (3), African Economic Research Consortium, 1991

Bascom, W. R., 'The Esusu: A Credit Institution of the Yorubu', *The Journal of the Royal Anthropological Institute*, LXXXII, (1), 1952, 63-70

Begashaw, G., 'The Economic Role of Traditional Savings and Credit Institutions in Ethiopia, *Savings and Development*, 2, (4), 1978, 249-262

Benedict, B., 'Capital, Saving and Credit among Mauritian Indians', *Capital, Saving and Credit in Peasant Societies*, ed. R. Firth and B. Yamey, 330-346, London, George Allen and Unwin, 1964

Berger, M., 'Giving Women Credit: The Strengths and Limitations of Credit as a Tool for Alleviating Poverty, *World Development*, 17, (7), 1989, 1017-1032

Besson, J., 'Women's Use of ROSCAs in the Caribbean: A Review', *Money-Go-Rounds: The Importance of ROSCAs for Women*, eds Shirley Ardener and Sandra Burman, Oxford, Berg Publishers, 1995

Biggs, T. F., Snodgrass, Donald R., and Srivastava, Predeep, 'On Minimalist Credit Programs', *Savings and Development*, 15, (1), 1991, 39-51

Bortei-Doku, E., and Aryeetey, E., 'Mobilizing Cash for Business: Women in Rotating *Susu* Clubs in Ghana', *Money-Go-Rounds: The Importance of RISCAs for Women*, eds Shirley Ardener and Sandra Burman, Oxford, Berg Publishers, 1995

Bouman, F.J.A., 'Indigenous Saving and Credit Societies in the Third World. A Message', *Savings and Development*, 1, (4), 1977, 181-218

----, 'The ROSCA: Financial Technology of an Informal Savings and Credit Institution in Developing Economies', *Savings and Development*, 3, (4), 1979, 253-276

----, 'Informal Savings and Credit Arrangements in Developing Countries: Observations from Sri Lanka', Adams et al, 1984, 222-247

----, *Small, Short and Unsecured: Informal Rural Finance in India*, Delhi, Oxford University Press, 1989

----, 'Informal Rural Finance. An Aladdin's Lamp of Inform-ation', *Sociologia Ruralis*, XXX, (2), 1990, 155-173

----, and Harteveld, K., 'The Djanggi, a Traditional Form of Saving and Credit in West Cameroon', *Sociologia Ruralis*, 16, (1-2), 1976, 103-118

----, and Houtman, R., 'Pawnbroking as an Instrument of Rural Banking in the Third World', *Economic Development and Cultural Change*, 37, (i), 1988, 69-89

----, and Moll, H.A.J., 'Informal Finance in Indonesia', *Informal Finance in Low-Income Countries*, ed. Dale Adams and D.A. Fitchett, 209-223, Boulder, Westview Press, 1992

Burman, S., and Lembete, N., 'Building New Realities: African Women and ROSCAs in Urban South Africa', *Money-Go-Rounds: The Importance of ROSCAs for Women*, eds Shirley Ardener and Sandra Burman, Oxford, Berg Publishers, 1995

Buvinic, M. and Berger, M., 'Sex Differentiation in Access to Small Credit Enterprise Development Fund in Peru', *World Development*,18, (5), 1990, 695-707

----, and Zeidenstein, S., *Credit for Rural Women some Facts and Lessons*, Washington D.C., Inter-national Center for Research on Women, 1979

Chandavarkar, A.G., 'The Non-Institutional Financial Sector in Developing Countries: Macroeconomic Implications for Savings Policies', *Savings and Development*, 9, (2), 1985, 129-174

Chilke, A. C., 'Rural Banking: a strategy for development in Nigeria - an appraisal', *Savings and Development*, 7, (1), 1983, 45-61

Chipeta, C., and Mkandawire, M.L.C., *The Informal Financial Sector and Macroeconomic Adjustment in Malawi*, African Economic Research Consortium, 1991, Research Paper 4

----, 'The Informal Financial Sector in Malawi', *Savings and Development* (Supplementary Issue 2), 1992, pp 121-154

Christen, R. P., 'Formal Credit for Informal Borrowers: Lessons from Informal Lenders', *Informal Finance in Low-Income Countries*, ed. Dale W. Adams and D.A. Fitchett, 281-292, Boulder, Westview Press, 1992

Coleman, J. S., *Foundations of Social Theory*, Harvard University Press, 1990

Cope, T., and Kurtz, D. V., 'Default and the Tanda: A Model Regarding Recruitment for Rotating Credit Associations', *Ethnology*, 19, (2), 1979, 213-231

Crowley, D. J., 'American Credit Institutions of Yoruba Type', reprint of article for *Man*, 1953

deLancey, M. W., 'Credit for the Common Man in Cameroon', *Journal of Modern African Studies*, 15, (2), 1977, 316-322

deLancey, V., 'Women at the Cameroon Development Corporation: How their Money Works: A Study of small-scale Accumulation of Capital by Women in Cameroon', *Rural Africana*, 2, 1978, 9-33

Due, J. M., and Summary, R., 'Constraints to Women and Development in Africa', *Journal of Modern African Studies*, 20 (1), 1982, 155-166

Dupuy, C., 'Le Secteur Financier Informel en Afrique de L'Oest', *Savings and Development*, (supplement 1), 1990, 15-33

Ezeabasili, A.N., 'The Ibo in Town and Tribe: Traditions and Beliefs of Nigeria's Second Largest Tribe', *African World*, April 1960, 8-12

Fernando, E., 'Informal Credit and Savings Organizations in Sri Lanka: the Cheetu system', *Savings and Development*, 10, (3), 1986, 253-262

Firth, R., and Yamey, B., eds *Capital, Saving and Credit in Peasant Societies: Studies from Asia, Oceania, the Caribbean and Middle America*, London, George Allen and Unwin Ltd, 1964

Fischer, B., 'Rural Financial Savings in Sri Lanka. Bottlenecks and Reform Proposals', *Savings and Development*, 12, (4), 1988, 35-60

Gabianu, S., *The Susu Credit System: An Indigenous Way of Financing Business Outside of the Formal Banking System*, Long-Term Perspective Study, Special Economics Office, World Bank, Technical Department, Africa Region, n.d.

Gedamu, F., 'Ethnic Associations in Ethiopia and the Maintenance of Urban/Rural Relationships: with special reference to the Alemgana-Wallamo Road Construction Association Associa-tion', Ph. D., University of London, 1972

Geertz, C., 'The Rotating Credit Association: A "Middle Rung" in Development', *Economic Development and Cultural Change*, 10, (iii), 1962, 241-263

Germidis, D., 'Interlocking the Formal and Informal Sectors in Developing Countries', *Savings and Development*, 14, (1), 1990, 5-21

Gomez, A., 'Women's Access to Credit in Latin America and the Caribbean', *United Nations International Research and Training Institute for the Advancement of Women*, 116-141, Santo Domingo, United Nations, INSTRAW, 1990

Haggblade, S., 'Africanization from Below: The Evolution of Cameroon Savings Societies into Western Style Banks', *Rural Africana*, 2, 1978, 35-55

Hamer, J. H., 'Preconditions and Limits in the formation of Associations: The Self Help and Cooperative Movement in Sub Sahara Africa', *African Studies Review*, 24, (1), 1981, 113-128

Harteveld, K., 'Savings and Credit in the Grassfields', M.Sc., Wageningen Agricultural University, 1972

Heald, S., 'Mafias in Africa: The Rise of Drinking Companies and Vigilante Groups in Bigisu District, Uganda', *Africa*, 56, (4), 1986, 446-465

Hendry, J., 'Tomodachi Ko: Age-mate Groups in Northern Kyushu', *Proceedings of the British Association for Japanese Studies*, 6, (2), 1981, 44-56

----, 'Women and Rotating Credit Associations in Japan', Unpublished paper given at The Centre for Cross-Cultural Research on Women, Queen Elizabeth House, Oxford, 1992

Holt, S. L., and Ribe, H., *Developing Financial Institutions for the Poor and Reducing Barriers to Access for Women*, World Bank, 1991, Discussion Paper 117

Hospes, O., 'Evolving Forms of Informal Finance in an Indonesian Town', *Informal Finance in Low-Income Countries*, ed. D.W. Adams and D.A. Fitchett, 225-238, Boulder, Westview Press, 1992a

----, 'People that Count: the Forgotten Faces of Rotating Savings and Credit Associations in Indonesia', *Savings and Development*, 16, (4), 1992b, pp 371-396.

----, 'Gender Differences in ROSCAs in Indonesia', *Money-Go-Rounds: The Importance of ROSCAs for Women*, eds Shirley Ardener and Sandra Burman, Oxford, Berg Publishers, 1995

----, De Groot, H. and Gerbrandy, A., 'NGOs Involved with Savings and Credit: (not) Making Strategic Choices?', Sri Lanka, 1988, unpublished

Ijere, M.O., 'Credit Development in Nigerian Agriculture', *Nigerian Journal of Economic and Social Studies*, 5, (2), 1963, 211-20

Illy, H.F., 'How to Build in the Germs of Failure: Credit Cooperatives in French Cameroun', *Rural Africana*, 2, Fall 1978, 57-67

Isong, G.N., 'Modernization of the Esusu Credit Societies', *Nigerian Institute of Social and Economic Research: Conference Proceedings*, Dec. 1959, 111-120

Izumida, Y., 'The Kou in Japan: A Precursor of Modern finance', *Informal Finance in Low-Income Countries*, ed. Dale W. Adams and D.A. Fitchett., 165-180, Boulder, Westview Press, 1992

Jerome, T.A., 'The Role of Rotating Savings and Credit Associations in Mobilizing Domestic Savings in Nigeria', *Savings and Development Supplement: African Review of Money, Finance and Banking*, 2, 1991, 115-125

Katzin, M., 'The Role of the Small Entrepreneur', *Economic Transition in Africa*, ed. M.J. Herskovits and M. Harwitz, 179-198, London, Routledge and Kegan Paul, 1964

Keim, S.M., 'Voluntary Associations among Urban African Women', *Culture Change in Contemporary African Communities from the African Field Center*, ed. B.M. Du Toit, Gainsville, Florida, University of Florida, 1970

Kerri, J.N., 'Studying Voluntary Associations as Adaptive Mechanisms: A Review of Anthropological Perspectives', *Current Anthropology*, 17, (1), 1976, 23-47

Khatib-Chahidi, J., 'Gold Coins and Coffee Parties in the Turkish Republic of Northern Cyprus: ROSCAs Coping with Inflation', *Money-Go-Rounds: The Imashingtonportance of ROSCAs for Women*, eds Shirley Ardener and Sandra Burman, Oxford, and , USA, Berg Publishers, 1995

Knez, E.I., 'Ke Mutual Aid Groups: Persistence and Change', 3, (n.d.)

Konig, W., and Koch, M., 'External Financing of Microenterprises in LDCs: Lessons from Colombia', *Savings and Development*, 14, (3), 1990, 233-246

Koufopoulou, S., 'Women and Rotating Credit Associations: Turkey', Unpublished conference paper given at the Centre for Cross-Cultural Research on Women, Queen Elizabeth House, Oxford, 1992

Kurtz, D.V., 'The Rotating Credit Association: An Adaptation to Poverty', *Human Organization*, 32/23, (1), 1973, 49-58

----, and Showman, M., 'The Tanda: A Rotating Credit Association in Mexico', *Ethnology*, 17, (i), 1978, 65-74

Ladman, J.R., and Adams, D.W., 'The Rural Poor and the Recent Performance of Formal Rural Sector Financial Markets in the Dominican Republic', *Canadian Journal of Agricultural Economics*, 26, (1), 1978

----, and Afecha, G., 'Group Lending: Why it Failed in Bolivia', *Savings and Development*, 14, (4), 1990, 353-366

Lamberte, M. B., 'Informal Finance in the Philippines' Footwear Industry', *Informal Finance in Low-Income Countries*, ed. Dale Adams and D.A. Fitchett, 133-147, Boulder, Westview Press, 1992

Lelart, M., 'Tontines et Tontiniers sur les Marches Africains: Le Marche Saint-Michel de Cotonou', *African Review of Money and Banking* 1989

Levin, D., *Susu and Investment in Trinidad*, Central Statistical Office, Trinidad, 1975, Research Paper 8

Lewis, B.C., 'The Limitations of Group Action among Entrepreneurs: the Market Women of Abidjan, Ivory Coast', *Women in Africa: Studies in Social and Economic Change* (eds) N.J. Hafkin and E.G. Bay, Stanford, Stanford University Press, 1976, pp 135-156

Light, I., *Ethnic Enterprise in America*, Berkeley, University of California Press, 1972

----, and Bonachiche, E., *Immigrant Entrepreneurs: Koreans in Los Angeles 1965-82*, Berkeley, University of California Press, 1988

----, and Deng, Z., 'Participation in ROSCAs within Korean Business Households in Los Angeles', *Money-Go-Rounds: The Importance of ROSCAs for Women*, eds Shirley Ardener and Sandra Burman, Oxford, Berg Publishers, 1995

Little, K.L., *African Women in Towns. An Aspect of Africa's Social Revolution*, Cambridge, Cambridge University Press, 1973

Lukhele, A. K., *Stokvels in South Africa: Informal Savings Schemes by Blacks for the Black Community*, Johannesburg, Amagi Books, 1990

Lycette, M., 'Improving Women's Access to Credit in the Third World: Policy and Project Recommendations', International Center for Research on Women, 1984

Madge, C., 'Intra-household use of income revenue and informal credit schemes in the Gambia', mimeo. 1991

Massengo, S., 'Women and Savings and Credit Associations', Unpublished paper given at The Centre for Cross-Cultural Research on Women, Queen Elizabeth House, Oxford, 1992

Mayoux, L., and Anand, S., 'Gender Inequality, ROSCAs and Sectoral Employment Strategies in the South Indian Silk Industry', *Money-Go-Rounds: The Importance of ROSCAs for Women*, eds Shirley Ardener and Sandra Burman, Oxford, Berg Publishers, 1995

Mbat, D. O., 'Savings Habit of Rural Households in Cross River State. An exploratory study', *Savings and Development*, 9, (4), 1985, 469-482

Mendez, K., 'Women's Access to Land as an Asset: an overview of the laws in 59 countries', *Credit Opportunities for Women of the Developing World*, 60-101, Santo Domingo, United Nations International Research and Training Institute for the Advancement of Women, 1990

Miracle, M. P., Miracle, D. S., and Cohen, L., 'Informal Savings Mobilization in Africa', *Economic Development and Cultural Change*, 28, (4), 1980, 701-724

Miyanaga, K., 'Economic *Kou* (ROSCAs) in Japan: A Review', *Money-Go-Rounds: The Importance of ROSCAs for Women*, eds Shirley Ardener and Sandra Burman, Oxford, Berg Publishers, 1995

Nafziger, E.W., *African Capitalism: a Study in Nigerian Entrepreneurship*, Stanford, California, Stanford University Press, 1977

Nayar, C.P.S., *Chit Finance: An Exploratory Study on the Workings of Chit Funds*, Bombay, Vora and Co., 1973

----, 'Can a traditional Financial Technology Co-exist with Modern Financial Technologies? The Indian Experience', *Savings and Development*, 10, (1), 1986, 31-58

----, 'Strengths of Informal Financial Institutions: Examples from India', *Informal Finance in Low-Income Countries*, ed. Dale Adams and D.A. Fitchett, 195-208, Boulder, Westview Press, 1992

Nelson, N., '"Women in Groups Can Solve their Problems Together". The Kiambu Group: A Successful Women's ROSCA in Mathare Valley, Nairobi (1971 to 1990)', *Money-Go-*

*Rounds: The Importance of ROSCAs for Women*, eds Shirley Ardener and Sandra Burman, Oxford, Berg Publishers, 1995

Newark, T., *Financial Markets: Developments in Sub-Sahara Africa. Discussion and Recommended Proposals*, Bureau for Africa, 1990, Working Paper

Ngozi, O.-I., 'Developing Financial Institutions in Nigeria's Rural Areas: Some Farm household Perspectives', *Savings and Development*, 6, (2), 1982, 169-193

Nguyen, van V., 'Savings and Mutual Lending Societies (ho)', Yale University, South East Asia Studies, 1949, mimeo

Niger-Thomas, M., 'Women's Access to and the Control of Credit through ROSCAs in Cameroon: The Mamfe Case', *Money-Go-Rounds: The Importance of ROSCAs for Women*, eds Shirley Ardener and Sandra Burman, Oxford, and Washington USA, Berg Publishers, 1995

Nwabughuogu, A. I., 'The Isusu: An Institution for Capital Formation among the Ngwa Ibo: Its Origins and Development to 1951', *Africa*, 54, (4), 1984, 46-58

Okonjo, K., 'Rural Women's Credit Systems: A Nigerian Example', *Studies in Family Planning*, 10, (11/12), 1979, 326-331

Osuntogun, A., and Adeyemo R., 'Mobilization of Rural Savings and Credit Expansion by Pre-Cooperative Organizations in South Western Nigeria', *Savings and Development*, 5, (4), 1981, 247-260

Padmanabhan, K.P., *Rural Credit: Lessons for Rural Bankers and Policy Makers*, London, IT Publications, 1988

Pastizzi-Ferencic, D., et al., *Women's Access to Credit in the Dominican Republic: a case study*, Vol. Supplement to News 15, UN Instraw, Instraw, UN, 1990

Ross, F., 'Strategies Against Patriarchy: Women and Rotating Credit Associations', B. Soc. Sci., Cape Town, 1990

Rowlands, M., 'Looking at Financial Landscapes: A Contextual Analysis of ROSCAs in Cameroon', *Money-Go-Rounds: The Importance of ROSCAs for Women*, eds Shirley Ardener and Sandra Burman, Oxford, and Washington, USA, Berg Publishers, 1995

Seibel, H.D. and Parhusip, U., 'Linking Formal and Informal Finance: the Indonesian Example', *Informal finance in Low-Income Countries*, (eds) D.W. Adams and D.A. Fitchett, Boulder, Westview Press, 1992, pp 239-248

----, and Shrestha, B., 'The Small Businessman's Informal Self-help Bank in Nepal', *Savings and Development*, 12, (2), 1988, 183-198

Sethi, R. M., 'Women's ROSCAs: Their Relevance in Contemporary Indian Society', *Money-Go-Rounds: The Importance of ROISCAs for Women*, eds Shirley Ardener and Sandra Burman, Oxford, and Washington USA, Berg Publishers, 1995

Shanmugan, B., 'Development Strategy and Mobilizing Savings through ROSCAs: The Case of Malaysia', *Savings and Development*, 13, (4), 1989, 351-367

----, 'Socio-economic Development through the Informal Credit Market', *Modern Asian Studies*, 25, (4), 1991, 209-225

Srinivasan, S., 'A Note on ROSCAs among South Asians in Oxford', *Money-Go-Rounds: The Importance of ROSCAs for Women*, eds Shirley Ardener and Sandra Burman, Oxford, and Washington USA, Berg Publishers, 1995

Strathern, M., *No Money on Our Skins: Hagen Migrants in Port Moresby*, Port Moresby, New Guinea Research Bulletin, 1975

Summerfield, H., 'A Note on ROSCAs among Northern Somali Women in the UK', *Money-Go-Rounds: The Importance of ROSCAs for Women*, eds Shirley Ardener and Sandra Burman, Oxford, and Washington, USA, Berg Publishers, 1995

Szabo, S., 'Rotating Credit Associations: Lessons for Development Strategy', Unpublished conference paper given at the Centre for Cross-Cultural Research on Women, Queen Elizabeth House, Oxford, 1992

Tebbut, M., *Making Ends: Pawnbroking and Working Class Credit*, London, Methuen, 1983

Timberg, T.A. and Aiyar, C.V., 'Informal Credit Markets in India', *Economic Development and Cultural Change*, 33, (1), 1984, 43-59

von Pischke, J.D., *Finance at the Frontier: Debt Capacity and the Role of Credit in the Private Economy*, EDI Development Studies, The World Bank, 1991

----, 'ROSCAs: State-of-the-Art Financial Intermediation', *Informal Finance in Low-Income Countries*, ed. dale W. Adams and D.A. Fitchett, 325-335, Boulder, Westview Press, 1992

Wainaina, N., *Indigenous Savings and Credit Schemes for Women in Kenya*, SIDA, 1989

Wu, D.Y., 'To Kill Three Birds with One Stone. The Rotating Credit Associations of Papua New Guinea Chinese', *American Anthropologist*, 1, (3), 1974, 565-584

## NAMES OF ROSCAS

*adashi* — Tiv, Nigeria
*adesa* - Ghana
*akpee* — Papua New Guinea
*arisan* — Tulehu, Molucca, Jakata
*asusu* — Gambia
*ban* — Nigeria
*bayanihin* — Philippines
*bia huey* — Thailand
*bishi* — India
*bisi* — Pakistan
*cheet* — Mauritius
*cheetu* — Sri Lanka
*chilemba* — Zimbabwe, Uganda, Zambia
*chiperegani* — Malawi
*chit fund groups* - India
*chita* or *chitu* among Indians and Tamils — South Africa
*chitties* — India
*consorcio* — Brazil
*cundina* — Mexico, California
*dashi* - Nigeria
*dhikur* — Nepal
*diaou monai* — Ivory Coast
*diddlums* — England
*djanggi* — Cameroon (variations are *jangi; ujangi*)
*djiji* — Ivory Coast
*donen ko* — Japan
*dushi* — Okinawa
*eqqub* — Ethiopia
*eso dzodzo* - Ghana
*esusu* — West Africa, Sierre Leone, Liberia (variations are *isusu, susu*)
*esu* — Bahamas
*gameya* — Egypt
*gooi-gooi* — South Africa
*hagbad* — Somalia
*hamamei* — Papua New Guinea
*ho* — Vietnam
*huis* — Korea, Taiwan, China
*ikelemba* — Zaire
*ikub* — Ethiopia also spelt *eqqub*
*iqqub* — Ethiopia
*junta* — Peru
*kameti* — India
*kampani* — New Guinea
*kate* — Japan
*ke* — Japan
*khatta* — Egypt
*kitemo* — Zaire
*knick-knack clubs* — England
*kongsi* - Borneo

*kootu* — Malaya, Singapore
*kou* — Japan
*ko* — Japan
*kuholisana* — South Africa
*kutu* — Malaysia
*kye* — Korea; Japan
*lae* — Papua New Guinea
*len chaer* — Thailand
*lun hui* — China
*mahodisana* and *stokfel* — Sudan, also South Africa
*mekim sande* — New Guinea
*menages* — Scotland
*mujin* — Korea
*nanamei akpee* — Ghana
*ndjonu* — Dahomey
*ngwa* — Cameroon
*njangi* — Cameroon
*nwega* — West Cameroon
*ofa*; *ofu* — Nigeria
*oha*; and *osusu* — West Africa
*osassa* — Zaire
*ossusu* — Nigeria
*otu*; *ota* — Nigeria
*otu-otu* — Nigeria
*padner, partner* — Jamaica
*paluwagan* — Malaya, Singapore
*paluwagin/paluwagen* — Philippines
*pandero* — Peru
*pasanakus* — Bolivia
*pati* — New Guinea
*pooling club* — South Africa
*safina mani* — Ivory Coast
*sande* — Papua New Guinea
*sandukem khattu* — Sudan
*sanduk* — Egypt
*san* — Dominican Republic
*stokvel* — South Africa, (variation *stockfel*)
*suit clubs* — Australia
*sundaying* — Papua New Guinea
*susu* — Trinidad
*tanda* — Mexico
*temo* — Zaire
*thukur* — Nepal
*tontine* — French-speaking West Africa — Senegal, Benin, also Malaysia and Singapore
*umgalelo* — South Africa
*ungalebo* — South Africa
*wari monai* — Ivory Coast
*xitique* — Mozambique

Note: this list is not exhaustive.

## ROSCAs: A Bibliography

Acharaya, M. 1990. Promotion of Linkages between Banks and Self-Help Groups in Nepal. Asian and Pacific Regional Agricultural Credit Association.
Not consulted.

Adams, D. W. 1992. Taking a Fresh Look at Informal Finance. In *Informal Finance in Low-Income Countries* (eds) D. W. Adams & D. A. Fitchett. Boulder: Westview Press pp. 5-23.
This is an introductory chapter to the book. ROSCAs are discussed on pages 13-14. Section 18-21 lists some lessons to be learned from informal finance.

Adams, D. W. & Canavesi de Sahonero, M. L. 1989. Rotating Savings and Credit Associations in Bolivia. *Savings and Development* 13 (3), 219-235.
The case study looks at ROSCAs in five Bolivian cities. One third or more of the population were found to be participants and 60% were women. A high proportion of those involved in the formal sector are participants. The paper describes three types of ROSCAs found. Some of the general points made here are very relevant to an assessment of ROSCAs.

Adams, D. W. & Fitchett, D. A. 1992. *Informal Finance in Low-Income Countries*. Boulder: Westview Press.
This is an interesting collection of essays many of which deal with ROSCAs. The contributors works are listed and annotated below.

Adams, D. W. & Ghate, P. B. 1992. Where to from Here in Informal Finance? In *Informal Finance in Low-Income Countries* (eds) D. W. Adams & D. A. Fitchett. Boulder: Westview Press, pp 349-359.
The author points out that out-of-date terminology stresses credit and not savings in the informal sector. There is much evidence to show the savings capacity of even very poor people. He stresses the strengths of the informal sector and sets out some research priorities. These include methodological issues, an attempt to seek generalizations which span countries; to identify desirable services provided by the informal sector; to study the way in which the informal sector avoids high transaction costs; to find a way to analyse borrowing costs (to include all expenses not just interest charges); and the interaction between the formal and informal markets. The discussion is important in terms of an assessment of ROSCAs.

Adams, D. W. & Nazarea-Sandoval, Virginia. 1992. Informal Finance in a Semi-Rural Area of the Philippines. *Savings and Development* 16 (2), 159-169.
The study is based on fieldwork and deals with the *paluwagan* (ROSCA). The 'pot' is distributed every fifteen days. There is consideration of the reasons why participants join ROSCAs. The bibliography lists a number of unpublished papers.

Adams, D. W., Graham, D. H. & von Pischke, J. D. 1984. *Undermining Rural Development with Cheap Credit*. Boulder, Colorado: Westview Special Studies in Social, Political and Economic Development.
A collection of essays which examine the reasons for the disappointing results of cheap loan programmes. Loan-recovery problems; discouragement of local savings; and the success of the rich in benefiting more than the poor are seen to be the result of well-intentioned but flawed policy. There are a number of case studies including Bouman's on Sri Lanka.

Adams, D. W. & Ladman, J. R. 1979. Lending to the Rural Poor through Informal Groups. A Promising Financial Market Innovation? *Savings and Development* 3 (2), 85-92.

The article looks at a number of experiments in lending to small farmers in 5 countries (in Latin America, Africa, Asia) and Turkey and mentions 7 others. Groups of 5-30 receive unsecured loans. They show that default risks have been reduced, as have loan transaction costs. Technical services have been introduced to accompany the loans. They consider the implications and potential of such schemes. There is no mention of ROSCAs but it is clear that the schemes described owe something to the ROSCA model.

Adeyemo, R. 1983. Credit as an Input in Marketing: a Study of the Nature and Use of Credit by Food Marketers in Anambra State of Nigeria. *Savings and Development* 7 (1), 63-73.
Data was obtained for 840 marketers—wholesalers and retailers– of several food crops. There are 4 sources of finance used for establishment capital—personal savings, *isusu*, family and friends, money-lenders. Results showed that 15.5% relied on *isusu* for start-up capital and 11.8% for working capital where borrowed money was involved. Other sources were available for working capital, for example commercial banks and co-operatives, trade associations and government agencies. The most popular source of loans is family and friends the least banks and government, 8.7% gave *isusu* as their preferred source of credit. Very little of *isusu* funds is spent on socio-religious activities now. Payment of school fees was the most important non-marketing use of loans. There is a discussion of interest rates.

Adeyeye, O. 1970. Cooperative Development through Adaptation: The Nigerian Experience. *Cooperative Information* 2. The author notes the hostility of cooperative officers to *susu*.

Adjetey, S. M. A. 1978. The Financial System In Ghana. Bank of Ghana, Research Department.
The author describes ROSCAs (known as *susu* clubs in Ghana) as thrift groups operated by market women and traders, and salaried workers in the urban centres. He refers to them as an important interest-free credit facility and 'widespread', but gives no indication of the extent of their presence anywhere in the country. The report also discusses other forms of informal credit and savings schemes.

Agabin, M., Lamberte, M., Mangahas, M. & Abrera-Mangahas. 1989. Studies on Informal Credit Markets in the Philippines (89-14). Philippine Institute for Development Studies, Manila. Not consulted.

Ahooja-Patel, K. 1990. Women's Inaccessibility to Credit: Problems and Policies. In *Women and Credit* (ed.) Santo Domingo: United Nations International Research and Training Institute for the Advancement of Women, pp 6-19.
The paper gives an overview of INSTRAW's research programme in the area of credit and women. It outlines the economic crises weighing down women, and the reasons why women form a small percentage of borrowers in developing countries. An analysis of the development plans of 96 countries showed that only 6 included women's occupations in investment targets. Attempts to examine women's non-access by separating demand from supply factors did not prove very fruitful. Fragmentary evidence available fails to pin-point the precise difficulties facing women in obtaining institutional loans. Examples are given from Peru and Jamaica. A section deals with self-reliant strategies, and women's repayment record. There are recommendations for policy actions at all levels. The discussion, while not dealing specifically with ROSCAs, goes some way to explaining the position of women in relation to credit.

Ahulu, N. H. 1988. The Nature and Characteristics of Informal Savings and Loan Associations. FAO/Ghana Workshop on Informal Financial Systems, Accra.
Ahulu discusses some of the dominant features of informal savings and loans associations, including the *susu* clubs, especially those that distinguish them from formal financial institutions. He describes the former as community-based and dependent on oral modes of transaction. Their resilience is attributed to accessibility and flexibility.

Almedom, A. M. 1991. *Aspects of the Growth and Health of the Suckling and Weaning Infant in Ethiopia*. Ph. D. Oxford.
There is description of the role of ROSCAs in providing an independent source of disposable income to the mother in times of the weaning of infants. Infants were given better quality weaning foods if the mother belonged to a ROSCA than if she did not.

Almedom, A. M. 1995. A Note on ROSCAs among Ethiopian Women in Addis Ababa and among Eritrean Women in Oxford. In *Money-Go-Rounds: The Importance of ROSCAs for Women* (eds) S. Ardener & S. Burman. Oxford & Washington, USA: Berg Publishers.
Almedom's paper is based on her field work of 1987-8 in Ethiopia on women and weaning patterns. She gives some background on the history of the country and stresses the repressive regime under which ROSCAs had survived. She draws on Gedamu's work as a framework for raising some of the important attributes of ROSCAs in the area. Her field work dealt with a sample of 113 women in the 18-43 age range from low income households: 68% of the sample belonged to ROSCAs, 18% of these groups were based on ethnicity and religious affiliations. She describes the social functions of the ROSCA— closely integrated with the coffee drinking ceremony, and stressed that no *quat* is chewed at these sessions. Some women's contributions are in fact paid by their husbands. A health link seems to exist between ROSCA membership of her sample and the purchase of higher quality weaning foods for infants. The second part of the paper concerns women from Addis Ababa living in Oxford. A group of women often dine together but also cater for their families at the meal. The role of hostess rotates and contributions of some £40 may be made.

Altaye, A. 1991. Mutual Assistance Network: The Case of Wolaite. Conference paper, XIth International Conference of Ethiopian Studies, Addis Ababa April 1-6.
Not consulted.

Ames, D. W. 1959. Wolof Cooperative Work Groups. In *Continuity and Change in African Culture* (eds) W. R. Bascom & M. J. Herskovitz. Chicago: University of Chicago Press.
Not consulted.

Amogu, O. O. 1956. Some Notes on Savings in an African Economy. *Social and Economic Studies* 5 (2), 202-209.
Amogu argues that native savings institutions deserve more attention from economists. He gives a number of reasons why people do not save with banks, and provides information of *isusu*. Some of these clubs function among mainly adolescent boys. He is critical of Bauer's 'West African Trade' which was published in 1954.

Anderson, R. T. 1966. Rotating Credit Associations in India. *Economic Development and Cultural Change* 14 (3), 334-339.
This work concerns *chit* funds in Hyderabad. The field work was carried out in 1962. Chit funds participants came from university staff as well as the poor. The author describes three types of funds: the simple, the common and the business *chit* fund. He refers to a village fund dating from 1950 and a business fund, which was legally registered and dated from 1951.

Anonymous 1992. The Kye System. *Asian American Market Report* 2, 2-3.
Not consulted.

Arax, M. 1988. Pooled Cash of Loan Clubs Key to Asian Immigrant Entrepreneurs. *Los Angeles Times*, 30 October, Sect. 2:1.
Not consulted.

Araya, L. 1984. *The Development of Savings and Credit Cooperatives in Ethiopia*, Addis Ababa: unpublished.
Chapter 4 deals with traditional savings associations.

Ardener, S. 1953. The Social and Economic Significance of the Contribution Clubs among a Section of the Southern Ibo. Conference Proceedings, N.I.S.E.R. Ibadan: The study stresses the crucial role of ROSCAs in the transformation from an agricultural to a trading economy. Groups with a membership of as many as 284 were found in the associations.

Ardener, S. 1964. The Comparative Study of Rotating Credit Associations. *The Journal of the Royal Anthropological Institute* **94** (Part 2), 201-228. Reprinted in Ardener and Burman 1995. This is a seminal work. It provides a definition of the associations, which is adopted by most other scholars. There is a wide-ranging account of the origins and geographical spread of ROSCAs, and a discussion of their importance. The article challenges some of Geertz's assumptions. It concentrates on a comparative institutional approach, raises some important issues and calls for further research. It provides a model questionnaire for the use of field researchers choosing to work on the subject.

Ardener, S. & Burman, S. 1995. *Money-Go-Rounds: The Importance of ROSCAs for Women.* Oxford & Washington, USA: Berg Publishers. The seventeen chapters in this book are referred to by author in this bibliography.

Aredo, D. 1991. *The Potentials of the Iqqub as an Indigenous Financing Small and Micro-scale Enterprises in Ethiopia.* The Hague, Sept 30- October 2: mimeo.
The paper begins with an overview of the Ethiopian economy. This includes a short treatment of the private sector, which survived in a generally hostile climate in small agriculture, passenger transport, and imports. There is a brief consideration of formal financial markets. The paper contains recent statistical data on Ethiopia, and some unpublished material. It also includes the results of very recent field research on *iqqubs*. The main part of the paper is discussion of the *iqqub*, identifying the different types; looking at the household characteristics of the participants; the characteristics of the rural *iqqub* and the links between them and the formal financial sector. The *iqqub* dates back to the Italian occupation. Some case studies are drawn from both urban and rural areas. A questionnaire was applied to a sample group at the University of Addis Ababa. The article ends with some consideration of the relevance of the *iqqub* to the promotion of small and micro scale enterprise. It adopts a sympathetic attitude to *iqqubs*. There is one mention of women's mutual support networks. There is a bibliography which includes a number of unpublished papers and reports.

Aryeetey, E. & Gockel, F. 1990. Mobilizing Domestic Resources for Capital Formation in Ghana: The Role of Informal Financial Credit Markets. African Economic Research Consortium, Nairobi.
The report identifies *susu* clubs as one of the commonest forms of informal savings in Ghana. It recognises the importance of *susu* clubs but notes that they may have been superseded in recent times by *susu* collectors engaged in mobile banking. The two forms of savings organization, however, co-exist in many parts of Ghana.

Aryeetey, E. & Gockel, F. 1991. Mobilizing Domestic Resources for Capital Formation in Ghana (3). African Economic Research Consortium.
The authors give an overview of the Ghanaian economy from 1974. Formal savings declined as interest in the informal sector quickened between 1976-84. Pages 8-11 give the results of a survey of 1000 market women, and show why they did not save with banks. The reasons given were low incomes, transaction costs in terms of time, banks' lack of interest in them, and the formality of banks. There are also political costs of dealing with banks. The number of market women who operated bank accounts fell by about 25% between 1982-90. Chapter 4 of the paper deals with the informal sector —informal savers and their backgrounds. There follows a discussion of *susu* clubs, and the rotating type is covered (pages 23-24; 28).

Asakura, K. 1961. *History of Financial Structure in Japan during the First Half Period of the Meiji Period (in Japanese)* Tokyo: Iwanami-Shoten.

The work is cited in Izumida (1992).

Asfaw, D. 1958. 'Equb'. *Ethnological Society, University of Addis Ababa, Quarterly Bulletin* **8**, 63-76.
The reference is cited in Aredo. It is the work of an anthropologist.

Asian Development Bank 1990. Informal Finance in Asia. In *Asian Development Outlook*, Manila: Asian Development Bank, pp 187-215.
Not consulted.

Aziz, R. 1977. The Role of Women in Banking and Rural Credit FAO.
Not consulted.

Bailey, L. 1990. Informal Financial Markets in Uganda: Potential Implications for Monetary Policy World Bank.
The author notes that very little work has been done on the topic for at least 15 years. She mentions *chilembas* and earlier reports of much smaller groups.

Bailey, L. E. 1990. Final Report: Informal Markets in Uganda-Potential Implications for Monetary Policy. Robert Nathan Associates Inc., Washington D. C.

Baker 1986. *The Rural-Urban Dichotomy in the Developing World: A Case Study from Northern Ethiopia*. Norwegian University Press.
This work is cited in Aredo; apparently it is an anthropological work and pays little serious attention to economic analysis.

Barnes, S. T. 1975. Voluntary Associations in a Metropolis: the case of Lagos, Nigeria. *African Studies Review* **XVIII** (2), 75-87.
The article covers a range of voluntary associations. Yoruba and Ibo have a higher participation rate than Hausa. Membership also varies according to socio-economic status and gender. There are statistics on membership of associations according to length of residence in the capital. Of a sample of 91 men 11% belonged to *esusu* and of 87 women 25% were members. These were all Yoruba; no Ibo were found to be members.

Barnes, S. T. & Peil, M. 1977. Voluntary Associations: Membership in Five West African Cities. *Urban Anthropology* **6**, 83-106.
Not consulted.

Barton, C. 1977. *Rotating Credit Associations and Informal Finance: Some Examples from South Vietnam*. San Diego: Asia, Vietnam.
Not consulted.

Bascom, W. R. 1952. The *Esusu*: A Credit Institution of the Yorubu. *Journal of the Royal Anthropology Institute* **LXXXII** (1), 63-70.
The author produces evidence to show that the ROSCAs are an ancient institution. He reviews the literature up to 1952, and describes how the associations work. He divides the ROSCAs into two groups—restricted and unrestricted. The former involve participants from the compound; either women of the compound or daughters of the compound. Men do not form ROSCAs within the compound. Unrestricted associations have an open membership and he found many of these in Ife. Many associations had no meetings. He also shows how they were open to corruption.

Begashaw, G. 1977. Ikub: the Rotating Credit Association in Ethiopia and its Role in the Mobilization of Savings. mimeo.
Not consulted.

Begashaw, G. 1978. The Economic Role of Traditional Savings and Credit Institutions in Ethiopia. *Savings and Development* **2** (4), 249-262.

This article draws almost entirely on secondary material. The *ikub*, is the type of ROSCA described in the article. It is estimated that in Addis Ababa, where banking facilities are extensive, 60% of the population are members of *ikubs*, and among craftsmen it may be as high as 90%. The association has economic and social functions. Men, women and even children may be members. Relatively little is known about how the funds are used. A participant may hold a fraction of a share in these organizations. The system used for determining who should receive the pay-out is the drawing of lots. The author sees ways in which capital may be transferred from the city to the village through the *ikub*. The author stresses the flexibility of the associations and the ease with which they may be adapted to meet modern needs while retaining some of their traditional characteristics. There is a survey of other types of community financial associations— *idir*, *mahaber*, church associations, mutual aid organizations and regional associations.

Bekolo-Ebe, B. & Bilongo, R. 1987. Liquidity, Intermediation and Savings Behaviour in Tontines. *Revue Camerounaise de Management* **6-7**, 90-105. Not consulted.

Belshaw, C. S. 1964. Institutions for Capital Formation and Distribution among Fijians. In *Capital, Saving and Credit in Peasant Societies* (eds) R. Firth, & B. Yamey. London: George Allen and Unwin Ltd. pp 187-206.

The article deals with credit unions, which were established in Fiji in 1954. There is mention of an earlier ceremonial borrowing, 'the scourge of Fiji' named *kerekere*, which is said to have all but died out. It is not clear whether there was a rotating element.

Benedict, B. 1964. Capital, Saving and Credit among Mauritian Indians. In *Capital, Saving and Credit in Peasant Societies* (eds) R. Firth & B. Yamey. London: George Allen and Unwin Ltd. pp 330-346.

The article is based on two years' field work. Various sources of borrowing are discussed, including a 'cycle' or *cheet*. Lots are drawn to determine who wins the cash. If the cycle is renewed the member who drew last on the first round draws first on the second. The Chinese on the island operate a slightly different system which involves interest payments for late drawers.

Bentil, J., Gadway, H., Monikes, V. & Schmidt, R. H. 1988. *Rural Finance in Ghana*. Interdisciplinaire Project Consult.

IPC describes the structure and operations of the *susu* clubs in some detail, noting that although they are informal they are regulated by strict codes of conduct. This reduces the risk for the participants. The document on the whole presents an extensive discussion of formal and informal savings in the rural areas.

Berger, M. 1989. Giving Women Credit: The Strengths and Limitations of Credit as a Tool for Alleviating Poverty. *World Development* **17** (7), 1017-1032.

The author notes that recently NGOs and other donors have taken to providing credit for women. She examines the effectiveness of different types of programmes, drawing examples from Colombia, Indonesia, Ecuador, El Salvador, India, and Bangladesh. There is some discussion of the constraints on women's access to formal credit and a mention of ROSCAs, which sees reliance on them as having a negative impact. Continued reliance on them is a means of marginalizing women's economic activity.

Bergstrom, T. 1986. Soldier of Fortune?. In *Equilibrium Analysis: Essays in Honour of Kenneth J. Arrow* (eds) W. P. Heller, R. M. Starr & D. A. Starrett. Cambridge: Cambridge University Press. This source is cited in two recent works on ROSCAs.

Berninghausen, J. & Kerstan, B. 1992. *Forming New Paths: Feminist Social Methodology and Rural Women in Java*. London: Zed Press.
Chapter 8 deals with *arisans* and co-operatives.

Besley, T. & Coate, S. 1991. Group Lending, Repayment Incentives and Social Collateral (132). Princeton N. J. Woodrow Wilson School.
Not consulted.

Besley, T., Coate, S. & Loury, G. 1990. The Economics of Rotating Savings and Credit Associations (149). Princeton, Woodrow Wilson School.
The paper draws upon the anthropological literature and uses a model to provide an economic analysis of the role and performance of ROSCAs, which are divided into two types; those which use random allocation (lots) and those which employ bidding in the allocation of funds. The ROSCAs are described as associations which are mainly used to allow the participant to purchase an indivisible good, and as being insignificant in terms of providing savings for old age. It assumes that members are unable to borrow in conventional money markets, and that they are relatively homogeneous. The paper discusses the sustainability of ROSCAs.

Besley, T., Coate, S. & Loury, G. C. 1990. The Economics of Rotating Savings and Credit Associations. London: Centre for Economic Policy Research.
This paper is cited in their later work.

Besson, J. 1995. Women's Use of ROSCAs in the Caribbean: A Review. In *Money-Go-Rounds: The Importance of ROSCAs for Women* (eds) S. Ardener & S. Burman. Oxford, & Washington, USA: Berg Publishers.
The paper draws on existing studies and literature on ROSCAs in the Caribbean. It has five sections, the first is a survey of the geographical spread of ROSCAs, e.g. Jamaica, Trinidad, Barbados, Guyana, Monserrat, Haiti, Martinique, St. Vincent, etc. The second section deals with the structure, organization and function of the clubs. Besson gives an historical perspective to the issue and mentions the local names for the associations which vary widely from isle to isle. There is speculation that they are derived from Yoruba tradition in some areas. The paper considers the role of women in ROSCAs and the interpretation of women's creative role in Caribbean culture.

Bhende, M. J. 1986. Credit Markets in Rural South India. *Economic and Political Weekly* XXI (38; 39).
Not consulted.

Biggs, T. F., Snodgrass, D. R. & Srivastava, P. 1991. On Minimalist Credit Programs. *Savings and Development* 15 (1), 39-51.
This is an analysis of two minimalist credit programmes, which lend small sums to the landless. The article is of interest to those concerned with ROSCAs because a number of features of these programmes are common to ROSCAs. The article looks at the main constraints on lending to the very poor—high transaction costs, considerable management effort, and the fact that the borrowers are very vulnerable to economic shocks, although they may be well-disposed to repay loans. The two case studies are the Grameen Bank in Bangladesh, established in 1983 (which gets concessionary funding) and the Badankredit Kecamatan in Java, which was set up in 1970.

Bonnett, A. W. 1976. *Rotating Credit Associations among Black West Indian Immigrants in Brooklyn: An Exploratory Study*. New York, City University.
Not consulted.

Bonnett, A. W. 1981. *Institutional Adaptation of West Indian Immigrants to America: an Analysis of Rotating Credit Associations* Washington D.C.: University Press of America Inc.
Not consulted.

Bortei-Doku, E. & Aryeetey, E. 1995. Mobilizing Cash for Business: Women in Rotating *Susu* Clubs in Ghana. In *Money-Go-Rounds: The Importance of ROSCAs for Women* (eds) S. Ardener & S. Burman. Oxford, & Washington, USA: Berg Publishers.

This paper describes *susu* and sets out to cover three aspects of ROSCAs: their resilience, the gender dimension, and changes in the operation of the clubs. Most of the available case studies have been of southern Ghana. The paper deals with two types of savings club —that with minimal organization and very few meetings which is very common in the rural areas; and the mutual aid *susu*, which has an emergency fund and is keen to be known for its mutual aid function. This type tends to be in the urban areas and to be wealthier than the rural ones. It seems clear that some societies begin as mutual aid associations and grow into savings societies. Motives for joining are predominantly economic but the survival of the groups depends upon mutual trust. The clubs have survived because their operating costs are very low, their structure simple and they are flexible. They represent a more formal version of the reciprocal arrangements that are common to the society as a whole. There is a homogeneous character to the clubs in terms of ethnic group, age group, occupation, educational level and gender. Women dominate the clubs in both rural and urban areas, but the 'government' clubs in the urban areas tend to be male dominated, while the market ones are run by women. There is very little difference in the use of funds by male and female members. Money goes as working capital and for educational provision. Changes which have taken place are the establishment of loan funds, and the emergence of the *susu* collector, who is usually a man.

Bouman, F. J. A. 1977. Indigenous Saving and Credit Societies in the Third World. A Message. *Savings and Development* 1 (4) 181-219.

The article examines traditional credit clubs and the ingredients of ROSCAs' success. It provides a useful list of the names of ROSCAs in different countries, looks at the development dimensions of the associations and discusses the reasons for government hostility.

Bouman, F. J. A. 1979. *Credit Informel dans l'economie Rurale des Pays en Voie de Developpment: Mythe et Realite.* Tunis: unpublished.
Not consulted.

Bouman, F. J. A. 1979. The ROSCA: Financial Technology of an Informal Savings and Credit Institution in Developing Economies. *Savings and Development* 3 (4), 253-276.

The author points to much evidence to refute the myth that the poor are unable to save. He describes the essential characteristics of the ROSCA, which he sees as an almost universal phenomena in the developing world. He points out that the socialising function of the ROSCA is disappearing in some countries (e.g. in Vietnam). In some countries foremen make rounds to collect the contributions and to make the payouts. The second section of the paper examines the advantages and disadvantages of the ROSCA. One of its strengths is that money is never left lying idle, others are that overhead costs are kept to a minimum, and there is little fraud. There is a discussion on the element of risk involved in the ROSCA. The commonly held view that much of the savings is spent on entertainment is challenged: a recent study of 25 *esusu* in Nigeria showed that less than 3% of the funds were spent in this way. Section 4 discusses the major criticisms of the ROSCA, and 5 the adaptation and evolution of the institution. This includes reference to the Indian *chit* fund. The article ends on a positive note about the strengths and adaptability of the institution.

Bouman, F. J. A. 1984. Informal Savings and Credit Arrangements in Developing Countries Observations from Sri Lanka. Adams *et al.*, 222-247.

There is a description of the *cheetu* system (ROSCAs) in the country, an account of the interest which the poor have in saving, and the reasons for their preference for the informal sector over the formal, in spite of good interest rates at the banks. Women outnumber men as players in the *cheetu*, but men usually pay the greater part of their wives' subscriptions, and women often substitute for men in having more than one stake in a *cheetu*. ROSCAs no longer have a socializing function; most are run by a business person.

Bouman, F. J. A. 1989. *Small, Short and Unsecured: Informal Rural Finance in India* Delhi: Oxford University Press.

The work discusses the role of the *bishi* (money club), one type of which is a ROSCA, which developed in Sangli after 1960 but which spread to many irrigated villages by the mid-1980s. The membership can be up to 100. The study covers farmers' organizations and milk distributors' *bishi* among others. The organizers are often merchants, and in some cases they had stopped holding formal regular meetings. The introduction of formal procedures - passbooks, etc. are a feature of some. Bouman also covers Urban Credit Societies (UCSs) which are mainly composed of farmers, are more formal and have done less well than the *bishis*.

Bouman, F. J. A. 1990. Informal Rural Finance. An Aladdin's Lamp of Information. *Sociologia Ruralis* XXX (2), 155-173.

The article, by one of the foremost scholars in the field on ROSCAs, challenges some common myths about informal finance. Misunderstandings are reviewed and explained, and the suggestion is made that there is a new approach towards the informal sector, partly as a result of the oil crisis. It argues that with a few exceptions in the aid sphere all the emphasis has been on loans not on savings. There has been a misunderstanding of informal finance, and a stereotyped picture of the moneylender. Top-down decision-making has led to a misallocation of funds. The article ends with a call for unbiased research and a new approach to the issues.

Bouman, F. J. A. & Bastiaanssen, R. 1992. Pawnbroking and Small Loans: Cases from India and Sri Lanka. In *Informal Finance in Low-Income Countries* (eds) D. Adams & D. A. Fitchett. Boulder: Westview Press, pp 181-194.

The article explains the popularity of pawnbroking for both lender and borrower. It touches on the failings of cheap loan policies. It deals with areas relevant to a study of ROSCAs.

Bouman, F. J. A. & Harteveld, K. 1976. The *Djanggi*, a Traditional Form of Saving and Credit in West Cameroon. *Sociologia Ruralis* 16 (1-2), 103-118.

This is a study of Babanki, a group of villages in the Grassfields region. The population numbered 4000 at the time of the study. The authors discuss the origins of the associations and the procedures. Entertainment and social functions are important characteristics of these ROSCAs. Contributions from participants may vary in size. Careful records are taken at meetings. The president has an unpaid role but it enhances his status. Many people belong to more than one organization so there are, in effect, overlapping rings of associations. There is not a very lengthy discussion of the use to which savings are put, but it does appear that consumption features large, and that the groups are popular for the building up of dowries. There are parallel associations, described as special or trouble funds for the use of members. Women have formed special corn mill associations. The authors stress the flexibility of the ROSCAs, their educative role and the fact that they have been recognized and incorporated in the extension programme of Peace Corps workers.

Bouman, F. J. A. & Moll, H. A. J. 1992. Informal Finance in Indonesia. In *Informal Finance in Low-Income Countries* (eds) D. Adams & D. A. Fitchett. Boulder: Westview Press, pp 209-223.

ROSCAs are dealt with on page 215. Some ROSCAs perform social functions and/or religious functions. The government and NGOs have involved *arisan* with their educational programmes, for issues like family planning, mother and child care. It was discovered that women are more likely to participate in these programmes if they are combined with *arisan*.

Bouman, F. J. A. & Houtman, R. 1988. Pawnbroking as an Instrument of Rural Banking in the Third World. *Economic Development and Cultural Change* 37 (i), 69-89.

The authors discuss the favourable features of informal lending in the Third World. Transaction costs are a key element in rural finance. The reasons for saving valuables, and the attraction of the pawnbroker are explained. There is data on Sri Lanka. The article ends with a discussion of the criticisms levelled against the informal market.

Brenner, G. A., Fouda, H. & Toulouse, J.-M. 1989. Projet Cameroon: les Tontines et la Creation d'Enterprises au Cameroun. Ecole des Hautes Etudes Commerciales, Centre D'Etudes d'Administration Internationale.
Not consulted.

Brown, D. & Korten, D. 1989. Understanding Voluntary Organizations: Guidelines For Donors (258). World Bank. Clearly of interest to NGOs but not consulted.

Burja, J. M. 1975. Women 'Entrepreneurs' of Early Nairobi. *Canadian Journal of African Studies* IX (2), 213-234.
Women, through prostitution or brewing, accumulated money which they invested in real estate, particularly Pumwani estate. There is a discussion of the role of welfare societies which the women founded; these were mainly Muslim. This deals with the same type of data as Nelson, see below, Nelson, N..

Burkins, D. 1984. *Waiting for Company: Development on the Periphery of the Southern Highlands Province, Papua New Guinea.* Temple University, Philadelphia.
The author in a survey of 24 households found that males were involved in *sande*, he reports no evidence for women.

Burman, S. & Lembete, N. 1995. Building New Realities: African Women and ROSCAs in Urban South Africa. In *Money-Go-Rounds: The Importance of ROSCAs for Women* (eds) S. Ardener & S. Burman. Oxford, & Washington, USA: Berg Publishers.
The paper deals with urban South Africa and draws upon interview material from field research and a 1993 commercial market research survey. The fieldwork data is from Cape Town and Johannesburg and includes information on how ROSCAs are being incorporated into the formal economy. The evidence seems to suggest that ROSCAs date from the early twentieth century or possibly earlier. A survey of 1300 individuals shows that 25% are in some type of mutual aid group, but ROSCAs account for less than one-sixth of this. Of those in ROSCAs, women in the 24-49 age group made up the majority (60%). Men dominate the larger and richer groups; some groups are for women only. Burman and Lembete discuss the criteria which exist for joining a club; the extent to which there is a social dimension to the ROSCAs, and the discipline imposed on members. Socializing is important and in the rich clubs in Johannesburg may involve dining in hotels. Pay-outs from the big clubs are put to 'serious use'. All those interviewed, except one, had bank accounts as well as belonging to ROSCAs. The ROSCAs were seen as a vehicle for upward social mobility for all classes. They are a way through which people adapt to new cultural trends and social mores. The value of ROSCAs in budgeting, as support groups and centres of information are evident. The groups are found among black African and Indian groups but not, as far as is known, among whites and coloureds.

Buvinic, M. & Berger, M. 1990. Sex Differentiation in Access to Small Credit Enterprise Development Fund in Peru. *World Development* 18 (5), 695-707.

Buvinic, M., et al. 1979. *Credit for Rural Women some Facts and Lessons*, Washington D.C., International Center for Research on Women.

Buysse, J. M. 1976. Het Cooperatieve Bankwezen in Kameroen. *Maandschrift Economie* 40 (7), 377-395.
Not consulted.

Callier, P. 1990. Informal Finance: The Rotating Saving and Credit Association : An Interpretation. *Kyklos* (Switzerland) 43 (2), 273-276.
Not consulted.

Campbell, C. D. & Chang, S. A. 1962. *Kyes* and *Mujins*: Financial Intermediaries in South Korea. *Economic Development and Cultural Change* 11 (1), 55-68.
*Kyes* unite members of primary groups, i.e. households. *Mujins* are business associations. The former began as associations catering for wedding and funeral expenses. The study draws on data from a 1959 household survey. It applies mathematical formula used for annuities to the associations. The rates of interest on *kye* long-term deposits are much higher than those paid by commercial banks. The author regards the *kye* as unsatisfactory organizations in that they are used for consumption purposes. The *mujins* grew rapidly between 1954 and 1959 and have been closely associated with the development of manufacturing. They were introduced by the Japanese and regulated by law in 1931. The growth of these has led to a fall in the popularity of *kyes*.

Ceesay-Marenah, C. 1982. Women's Cooperative Thrift and Credit Societies. In *Women and Work in Africa* (ed.) E. G. Bay. Boulder, Colorado: Westview, pp 289-295.
The article stresses the importance of the savings movement among women in Gambia, but it is concerned with co-operatives rather than ROSCAs.

Central Bank of Japan 1961. Survey of *Mujin*-Companies. *Documents of Financial History in Japan* 25 (in Japanese)
Not consulted.

Central Statistical Office, 1982. Statistical Abstract (Ethiopia) Addis Ababa, Central Statistical Office.
The national rural household statistical survey collected data on savings and *iqqub*. The proportion of annual household income allocated to *iqqub* was found to be 0.96% according to Aredo. Case studies are documented.

Chandavarkar, A. G. 1985. The Non-Institutional Financial Sector in Developing Countries: Macroeconomic Implications for Savings Policies. *Savings and Development* 9 (2), 129-174.
The paper analyses the macroeconomic implications of non-institutional financial sectors in developing countries and suggests ways of strengthening links with the formal sector. Only in Latin America are the formal institutions used more than the informal ones. The article looks at the nature and character of the non-institutional sector; lists names of ROSCAs and the uses to which funds are put.

Chem-Langhee, B. 1989. *Traditional and Modern Modes of Cooperation in Nso*. Research Report 35/1989, eds. P. Geschiere and P. Konigs, African Study Centre, Leiden.
This provides some historical background about changes in cooperative labour effort to meet new economic possibilities. The early *ngwa* (plural *angwa*) were labour centred. Later drinking clubs became prominent. Originally the clubs were exclusively male, now all except some associated with former military lodges are open to both sexes. There is some data on the procedures and the use made of savings: school fees and taxes. In the towns the associations have become more formal and various types of funds have been established.

Chilke, A. C. 1983. Rural Banking: a strategy for development in Nigeria - an appraisal. *Savings and Development* 7 (I), 45-61.
The article looks at the record of co-operative banks in the rural sector, which are viewed as competing with the commercial banks and failing the co-operatives. Inadequacies of institutional sources of credit have left the agricultural sector reliant on informal finance. Sources are quoted which bear this out. There is reference to the importance of ROSCAs in other societies, India, Ethiopia, but no data given on Nigeria. The author does point to the enormous potential of reserves of financial resources in the country which could be more productively utilized. He advocates an extension of the banking service, suggesting Brazil and India as models, and examines the country's record to date in the provision of services in the rural areas.

Chipeta, C. & Mkandawire, M. L. C. 1992. The Informal Financial Sector in Malawi. *Savings and Development* (Supplementary Issue 2) pp 121-154
The authors describe Co-operative Savings Associations which seem to have the characteristics of ROSCAs, but they object to the use of the term. In fact they find the terms 'credit' and 'rotation' objectionable. The local terms are *chiperegani* and *chilimba*. These associations are not recognized by law. It seems that these associations can not cater for all the needs of members. The authors point out their limitations.

Chira, S. 1987. It's Clubby, It's Thrifty, and It Can Cover the Bills. *New York Times*, 19 November, Sect 1:4.
Not consulted.

Chotigeat, T. 1985. *Heuy* in Thailand. *Journal of Economic Development* **10** (2).
Not consulted.

Chotigeat, T. 1987. Savings Mobilization via Rotating Savings and Credit Societies in LDCs. World Bank.
Not consulted.

Christen, R. P. 1992. Formal Credit for Informal Borrowers: Lessons from Informal Lenders. In *Informal Finance in Low-Income Countries* (eds) D. W. Adams & D. A. Fitchett. Boulder: Westview Press, pp 281-292.
Micro-credit development programmes are too expensive because they copy the formal banking sector. If they are to be successful they should follow the methods of the informal sector which have financed small businesses since the beginning of time. The article draws on the experience of ACCION International's experience in Latin America over an 18 year period. It has evolved a credit model based on those of the informal sector. The loan recovery rate has been extremely successful (99.5%). The article identifies six lessons learned from traditional moneylenders—know your borrowers; do not supervise loans; take loans to the client; provide adequate credit; charge commercial rates and be tough with defaulters.

Comhaire, S. 1966. *Wage Pool as a Force of Voluntary Association in Ethiopia and other African Towns*. Haille Selassie University.
Not consulted.

Cope, T. & Kurtz, D. V. 1979. Default and the Tanda: A Model Regarding Recruitment for Rotating Credit Associations. *Ethnology* **19** (2), 213-231.
The authors adopt an approach to ROSCAs which is not just an economic one. The article is based on research in Puebla, Mexico in 1976. In this area the associations are called *tanda*. They carried out interviews and administered a questionnaire to see what type of people were most likely to join a *tanda*. They found that gender and religion were not helpful guides as to who joined. Males with two jobs were more likely to join than those with only one.

Coplan, D. R. 1979. *The Stokvel: Rotating Credit Associations and Social Adaptation*. Cincinnati, Indiana University: unpublished.
Not consulted.

Crowley, Daniel J.,1953. American Credit Institutions of Yoruba Type, brief reprint of article for *Man*.
The author, commenting on Bascom's work, states that the Yoruba type of ROSCA existed in the Bahamas, where it is known as *esu* ; in Trinidad and British Guiana, and possibly in Jamaica and Florida. He writes that Bahamian workers returning from the United States claimed that there were many *esu* in Florida, and that 'American negroes' are joining and setting up associations of their own.

Cuevas, C. E. 1991. *Financial Markets in Rural Zaire: An Assessment of the Bandundu and Shaba Regions (executive summary)* Ohio: Ohio State University.
The traditional view of informal financial intermediaries being exploitative and usurious is not supported by the findings from Zaire. This has implications for those concerned with ROSCAs.

deLancey, M. W. 1977. Credit for the Common Man in Cameroon. *Journal of Modern African Studies* 15 (2), 316-322.
The article is concerned with Credit Unions, which were first established in 1966 in Bamenda by a Roman Catholic priest. The author argues that the most important reason for their take off was the prior existence of ROSCAs. The significance of *njangis* is discussed; the origins of which are seen to be the traditional reciprocal labour arrangements for land clearance. The distinction between *njangis* and 'meetings' is explained, the latter are less traditional and are common among migrants.

deLancey, M. W. 1978. Institutions for the Accumulation and Redistribution of Savings among Migrants. *The Journal of Developing Areas* 12, 209-224.
The migrant workers in Cameroon have a good savings record. Some of this saving takes place through ROSCAS, other through 'meetings' of members of the same ethnic group who contribute to other types of saving funds. The author has done field work in the southwestern part of the country; he describes the *njangi*.

deLancey, M. W. 1978. Savings and Credit Institutions in Rural West Africa: An Introduction. *Rural Africana* 2, 1-7.
The author quotes Lugard in saying that Africans do not save. He provides an introduction to some of the literature on West Africa.

deLancey, M. W. 1987. Women's Cooperatives in Cameroon: the Cooperative Experiences of the Northwest and Southwest Provinces. *African Studies Review* 30 (1), 1-18.
This paper makes a passing reference to ROSCAs and comments on the weakness of the women's cooperative movement in Cameroon. Existing cooperatives in the southwest for women date only to 1970, and they constitute only a small portion of the movement. In the northwest they have a longer history. The history of both has been disappointing. The conclusions of the paper examine reasons for this. Lack of capital is seen to be one. ROSCAs are mentioned as one source of credit. Other problems have been those of poor education, leadership, conflict with well-established commercial interests, and hostility from men. There is a discussion of the importance of the weakness of the profit motive.

deLancey, V. 1978. Women at the Cameroon Development Corporation: How their Money Works: A Study of small-scale Accumulation of Capital by Women in Cameroon. *Rural Africana* 2, 9-33.
The article discusses the possibility of women saving, which is enhanced through wage labour with the Cameroon Development Corporation. There is a survey of the consumer durables bought. The writer found that wage earning women were able to save more, and that their savings were designed for educational purposes. The savings motives between wage earners and non-wage earners were different. There is a break-down of preferences of savings institution, and figures on the volume of savings placed with *njangis*, meetings and credit unions.

deLancey, V. 1978. Credit Union Activities in Cameroon. An example of an untapped source of investment fund. Paper presented at the Annual Conference of the SEA, Washington D.C.
Not consulted.

Derby, J. 1983. The Role of the Tanomoshi in Hawaiian Banking. *Social Process in Hawaii*, 30, 66-84.
Not consulted.

Devereux, S. & Pares, P. 1987. *A Manual of Credit and Savings for the Poor of Developing Countries.* OXFAM.
There is very little on ROSCAs, just a brief mention of Cameroon. A simple, clear outline of various factors relating to creditworthiness, the lack of access to loans of the poor because of illiteracy, distance factors, income instability, prejudice, administrative cost etc. German aid agencies have produced studies of a more detailed type.

Dewey, A. 1964. Capital, Credit and Saving in Javanese Marketing. In *Capital, Saving and Credit in Peasant societies. Studies from Asia, Oceania, the Caribbean and Middle America.* (eds) R. Firth & B. Yamey. London: George Allen and Unwin Ltd. pp 230-255.
Pages 253-254 deal briefly with *arisan*. Most of the money saved through the *arisan* is invested in trading. The *arisan* is described as fairly simple in procedures compared to some found elsewhere in Asia. They rotate endlessly with much the same membership but with relatively short cycles, and so inflation does not erode members' savings significantly if they are late in turn to receive the kitty.

Dievot, v. G. & Verboven, D. forthcoming. *Tussen Kulturele Traditie en Verandering: de Bamileke-tontine.* Ghent: University of Ghent.
Not consulted.

Djambou, G. 1970. *Le Tontine et du Meilleure dans le Developpment Economique et Social du Departement du Haut-Nkam* Doula: Institute Pan Africain pour le Developpment.
Not consulted.

Donald, G. 1976. *Credit for Small Farmers of Developing Countries* Colorado: Westview Press.
There is a brief mention of ROSCAs, named *huis* in Taiwan and Korea.

Due, J. M. 1991. Experience with Income Generating Activities for Southern African Women. *Savings and Development* 15 (1), 79-90.
This considers the credit needs of women in general, and the constraints which they face.

Due, J. M., Kurwijila, R., Aleke Dondo, C. & Kogo, K. 1990. Funding Small Scale Enterprises for African Women: Case Studies in Kenya, Malawi and Tanzania. *African Development Review* 2 (2), 58-82.
The article considers the role of NGOs, group loans and co-operatives. There is mention of reciprocal credit in cash or kind in Tanzania. All the women in the credit programme wanted more education about credit and loans.

Due, J. M. & Summary, R. 1982. Constraints to Women and Development in Africa. *Journal of Modern African Studies* 20 (1), 155-166.
The first part of the article is concerned with education. The second part is concerned with capital. Material is drawn from studies of the Zambia Agricultural Finance Company and the Sudan. There is a brief mention of ROSCAs on p. 163 which points out that, in Africa, there are as many as 22 names for ROSCAs.

Dupuy, C. 1990. Le Secteur Financier Informel en Afrique de L'Oest. *Savings and Development (supplement)* 1, 15-33.
The article looks at the strength and dynamism of the informal sector and village associations which he attributes, in part, to the failure of the state.

Eldjik, A. v. 1992. Private Interest Government through Spot Markets in West African Food Trade. In *Law as a Resource in Urban Studies* (eds) F. v. Benda-Beckmann & M. v. der Velde, Wageningen, Netherlands: Pudoc Publishers.
This article is cited by Dutch scholars, it concerns ROSCAs.

Embree, J. 1946. *A Japanese Village: Suye Mura* London: Kegan Paul.
The writer describes Japanese ROSCAs called *ko* or *kate*. The book explains the various terms used which relate to the form savings take and whether they are a bidding or a lottery type. (Savings may take the form of money or rice.) All large money *kogin* are registered, the semi-registered category have guarantors, and only the very small ones are not registered. The ROSCAs are usually set up by a person in need of a loan. They may last 20 years or more. Pages 108-117 deal with the *ko*.

Embree, J. K. 1939. New and Local Kin Groups among Japanese Farmers of Kona, Hawaii. *American Anthropologist* **41**, 400-407.
Not consulted.

Ezeabasili, A. N. 1960. The Ibo in Town and Tribe: Traditions and Beliefs of Nigeria's Second Largest Tribe. *African World* **April**, 8-12.
This work is cited in Katzin (1964).

FAO/APRACA 1985. *Mobilization of Rural Savings in Selected Countries in Asia and the Pacific* Bangkok: FAO.
Not consulted.

Fei, H.-T. 1946. *Peasant Life in China* New York, London: Routledge and Kegan Paul.
Pages 267-274 deal with *hui* in Shanghai. It is summarized by Geertz. A person wishing to obtain a loan will establish a *hui*. The kinship group is central to membership of the *hui*.

Fernando, E. 1986. Informal Credit and Savings Organizations in Sri Lanka: the Cheetu system. *Savings and Development* **10** (3), 253-262.
Even in a poor country where half the population receive food aid savings stamps there is great interest in saving. One of the principal attractions of ROSCAs is the enforced savings aspect. The government's Cheetu Ordinance No. 61 (1935) for the registration and control of *cheetus* is largely ignored by the people.

Fernando, N. A. 1992. Informal Finance in Papua New Guinea; An Overview. In *Informal Finance in Low-Income Countries* (eds) D. W. Adams & D. A. Fitchett. Boulder: Westview Press, pp 129-131.
The paper provides an overview of the informal financial sector in the country. ROSCAs (*sande*) seem to be a post 1960s phenomenon. The author found that almost all public sector institutions in Port Moresby had ROSCAs. They are found mainly among school teachers and low income groups however. The paper quotes other work which show where *sande* are found and that women are members. The article is repetitive.

Firth, R. 1964. Capital, Saving and Credit in Peasant Societies: A Viewpoint from Economic Sociology. In *Capital, Saving and Credit in Peasant Societies* (eds) R. Firth & B. S. Yamey. London: George Allen and Unwin Ltd, pp 15-34.
Pages 31-32 mention ROSCAs: *esusu* among the Yoruba. The author doubts if they can contribute very substantially to capital formation to promote economic growth.

Firth, R. & Yamey, B. 1964. *Capital, Saving and Credit in Peasant Societies: Studies from Asia, Oceania, the Caribbean and Middle America*. London: George Allen and Unwin Ltd.
This collection contains detailed essays on peasant economies several of which deal with ROSCAs or mention them in passing. In the conclusion Yamey suggests that economists' limited preoccupations have meant that they have forged few links with anthropologists and other social scientists. This is a disadvantage to them. He pleas for the economists to study the indigenous rural sector.

Fischer, B. 1988. Domestic Capital Formation, Financial Intermediation and Economic Development in Peru. *Savings and Development* **12** (4), 321-341.
The author mentions the widespread use of the ROSCA, known as *junta* or *pandero*, but the article is concerned in the main with government policy and interest rates, reasons for Peru's poor performance in mobilizing savings and for capital flight.

Gabianu, S. (n. d.). The *Susu* Credit System: An Indigenous Way of Financing Business Outside of the Formal Banking System. Long-Term Perspective Study, Special Economics Office, World Bank, Technical Department, Africa Region.
Gabianu comments on the welfare functions of the *susu* clubs.

Gamble, S. D. 1944. A Chinese Mutual Savings Society. *Far Eastern Quarterly* **4**, 41-52.
This early reference is cited by Ardener who is citing Geertz.

Gamble, S. D. 1954. *Ting Hsein: A North China Rural Community* New York: New York Institute of Pacific Relations.
Pages 260-271 mention savings associations. This is based on fieldwork of 1931.

Gedamu, F. 1972. *Ethnic Associations in Ethiopia and the Maintenance of Urban/Rural Relationships; with special reference to the Alemgana-Wallamo Road Construction Association.* University of London.
Gedamu details the functions of the different types of voluntary associations - economic, social, cultural and political in Imperial Ethiopia. This study is one of the most detailed on rotating credit associations in Ethiopia.

Geertz, C. 1962. The Rotating Credit Association: A 'Middle Rung' in Development. *Economic Development and Cultural Change* **10** (iii), 241-263.
The article looks at developments in Japan, India, China, Vietnam, Africa and Java. It is only for Java that he has original research data. Fieldwork was carried out in 1952-54. He deals with the *arisan* in Java in the rural areas and in towns. Urban *arisan* are especially popular among women. There are notable differences between the rural and urban associations; the latter incorporate a gambling element. One section of the urban ROSCAs are the business associations which have lost their social features and which have no meetings. The material on China is drawn from several sources including Gamble's on Peking. The Japanese *ko* bears some relation to the *arisan* according to his data. There is some material on the *ho* in Vietnam and on Ghana. The discussion of the role of the ROSCA in economic development is Geertz's main contribution to the debate about ROSCAs which has been followed up intermittently by economists.

Germidis, D. 1990. Interlocking the Formal and Informal Sectors in Developing Countries. *Savings and Development* **14** (1), 5-21.
A major focus of the paper is on policy attitudes and recommendations. It outlines two main approaches to the problem of dualism in the financial sector, one would require major reforms in the formal sector as a remedy; the other would mean the development of links between the two sectors. The author suggests a middle of the road policy — integration and inter-linkage simultaneously. He highlights the importance of the 'social insurance' characteristics of the informal sector and recommends building on this to reduce dualism.

Ghate, P. 1986. Some Issues for the Regional Study on Informal Credit Markets. Asian Development Bank.
This is cited in Hospes.

Ghate, P. 1990. Informal Finance: Some Findings from Asia. Unpublished paper for Asian Development Bank.
This is cited in Hospes.

Glacken, C. J. 1955. *The Great Loochoo: A Study of Okinawan Village Life*. Berkeley, California: University of California Press.
Pages 78-84 deal with ROSCAs.

Gomez, A. 1990. Women's Access to Credit in Latin America and the Caribbean. In *United Nations International Research and Training Institute for the Advancement of Women* (ed.) Santo Domingo: United Nations, INSTRAW, pp 116-141.
This is a discussion of the role of credit in women's development. There is an overview of the role of women in the labour force, and the role of women's income in poor households. This is followed by an examination of women's access to credit in the formal sector, and the importance of the informal sector - family, friends, pawnbrokers, wholesalers, etc. There are case studies of the Dominican Republic, Salvador, Nicaragua and Ecuador.

Government of India (1931). *The Indian Central Banking Enquiry Committee: Part I, Majority Report*. Calcutta, Government of India. There is valuable data of an historical nature in this report, cited in Sethi (below).

Government of Kerala. (1972). *The Kerala 'Chitties' Bill*. Government of Kerala.
Not consulted.

Grossman, R. 1989. *Deposit Insurance, Regulation, and Moral Hazard in the Thrift Industry: Evidence from the 1930s*. mimeo.
Mentioned by Besley, Coate and Loury (1990). Many US savings and loans institutions seem to have started as ROSCAs.

Haggblade, S. 1978. Africanization from Below: The Evolution of Cameroon Savings Societies into Western Style Banks. *Rural Africana* **2**, 35-55.
The study deals with urban associations. Migrants to the cities bring their rural savings and they set up ROSCAs. In the cities the associations are larger, multi-ethnic, and more sophisticated than in the rural areas. They keep written loan accounts, have collateral requirements and make interest charges. In 1975 business men set up the Banque Unie de Credit. The author views this as an evolution of the credit associations. There is an historical account of the development of urbanization and monetization in the country, and a distinction between rural and urban ROSCAs. Finally there is a discussion of the limits to the growth of the size of an association, the policy implications.

Hamalian, A. 1974. The Shirkets: Visiting Patterns of Armenians in Lebanon. *Anthropological Quarterly* **47** (1), 71-92.
Not consulted.

Hamer, J. H. 1981. Pre-conditions and Limits in the formation of Associations: The Self-help and Cooperative Movement in Sub-Sahara Africa. *African Studies Review* **24** (1), 113-128.
Cultural homogeneity and a limited number of social rules are insufficient for the formation of voluntary associations. There is a general discussion of the conditions necessary for the organization of self-help movements. Self-help groups are seen to have eased the strain of transition and the contradictions involved in the change from essentially tribal and/or colonial systems to independent nation states. Individualism and corruption have been constraints on the development and success of the associations.

Harteveld, K. 1972. *Savings and Credit in the Grassfields*. Wageningen Agricultural University.
Not consulted.

Heald, S. 1986. Mafias in Africa: The Rise of Drinking Companies and Vigilante Groups in Bigisu District, Uganda. *Africa* **56** (4), 446-465.

The work is based on fieldwork carried out in 1965-69 and in 1981. The author views the development of the two kinds of clubs, drinking and vigilante, to the lawlessness and anarchy of the country and sees some similarities with nineteenth century Sicily. Drinking clubs were set up for security - to regularize beer drinking - and evolved into credit organizations. The first officials were from the cotton and coffee co-operatives. The clubs are seen as a means of re-establishing traditional values by formalizing simple structures of reciprocity. By 1981 they were central to the 'black-market' economy.

Hellman, E. 1934. The Importance of Beer Brewing in an Urban Native Yard. *Bantu Studies* **8**, 34-60.
Hellman provides some of the earliest references to *stokvels*, which she did not think would survive.

Hellman, E. 1935. *Rooiyant: A Social Survey of an Urban Native Slum Yard*. Cape Town: Oxford University Press.
This is substantially the same as the 1934 reference listed above.

Hendry, J. 1981. Tomodachi *Ko*: Age-mate Groups in Northern Kyushu. *Proceedings of the British Association for Japanese Studies* **6** (2), 44-56.
The article is concerned with a range of age set groups. Various forms of mutual aid are discussed, some of which are rotating. Mothers form groups for young children and these are divided by sex. Regular savings are collected, originally for the purpose of making a pilgrimage to Mount Hiko, in the case of boys. The girls' groups meet less frequently, usually three times a year, on ceremonial occasions. Adult groups are also described.

Hendry, J. 1992. Women and Rotating Credit Associations in Japan. Paper presented at Centre for Cross-Cultural Research on Women workshop, Queen Elizabeth House, Oxford unpublished.
The author stresses that there is very little documentation of ROSCAs in Japan in the present era, but the work of the Embrees, describes what appears to be the classic type of ROSCA. There is little evidence of these in Japan now. A strong tradition of mutual support and reciprocity exists. The paper describes the religious origins of groups which save money for foreign travel (they originally saved for pilgrimages). There are age set savings groups formed by mothers on behalf of young children, groups for labour exchange—especially for house building. Other associations exist which may have evolved from ROSCAs, notably arrangements for access to funeral and wedding equipment, and housewives' bulk purchasing co-operatives. The later, however, lack the rotating element.

Herskovits, M. & Herskovits, F. 1947. *Trinidad Village* New York: Knopf.
Pages 76-77 describe a Trinidadian mutual credit society known as *susu*. The organizer is called the 'captain', and the payout 'the hand'.

Heyzer, N. 1990. Increasing Women's Access to Credit in Asia. Achievements and Limitations. In *Credit Opportunities for Women of the Developing World* (ed.) Santo Domingo: INSTRAW, pp 103-115.
The paper presents some success stories of credit assistance and self-help schemes in the rural areas of Asia. All involve the formal sector. The last part of the paper looks at the limitations of the schemes and makes some general recommendations.

Hill, P. 1970. *Studies in Rural Capitalism in West Africa*. Cambridge: Cambridge University Press.
Not consulted.

Hill, P. 1982. *Dry Grain Farming Families: Hausaland (Nigeria) and Karnataka (India) Compared*. Cambridge: Cambridge University Press.

Pages 216-223 examine rural credit schemes. It was found that in Batagarawa (near Katsina, Nigeria) all the conveyors and nearly all members of the schemes were women.

Holst, J. 1990. Personal Savings and Financial Development, Policies and Prospects. *Savings and Development* 14 (4), 313-350.
The article looks at two banks concerned with serving small customers - the rural banks in Ghana and the Grameen Bank in Bangladesh. There has been a rapid rise in savings and loans are granted on the reputation of the borrower rather than on collateral. Malaysia has tried to imitate the Grameen system with good results. Holst argues that there is scope for more replicas in Africa.

Holst, J. V. 1985. The Role of Informal Financial Institutions in Mobilizing Savings. In *Savings and Development, Proceedings of a Colloquium* (eds) D. Kessler & P. A. Ullmo. Paris: Economica Press, pp 121-152.
Not consulted.

Holt, S. L. 1991. *Village Banking: A Cross-Country Study of a Community-Based Lending Methodology*. Draft for World Bank's Women in Development Division and USAID GEMINI program, unpublished.
The study examines the Foundation for International Community Assistance (FINCA) model.

Holt, S. L. & Ribe, H. 1991. *Developing Financial Institutions for the Poor and Reducing Barriers to Access for Women* (117). World Bank.
The paper is an extended version of research done for the 1990 World Bank Development Report. It acknowledges that the experience of subsidized credit has been dismal, and that credit itself cannot generate income. Reform of financial sectors will not automatically provide better access for the poor, especially women. There is material on the informal sector, including ROSCAs (pp.x-xi), with detail on Ghana. It considers how donors and governments might try to copy successful informal systems or spread information about them. There is a section on successful delivery models. There are words of caution about interventionalist programmes for ROSCAs, and a call for more general research.

Hospes, O. 1988. *Policy Guidelines for NGOs involved in Saving and Credit Schemes* The Hague: NOVIB.
Not consulted.

Hospes, O. 1991. The Struggle for Cooperatives. In *The Struggle for Law* (eds) F. v. Benda-Beckman, et. al. Wageningen: Pudoc Publishers.

Hospes, O. 1992. Evolving Forms of Informal Finance in an Indonesian Town. In *Informal Finance in Low-Income Countries* (eds) D. W. Adams & D. A. Fitchett. Boulder: Westview Press, pp 225-238.
The article describes the situation in Tulehu in 1989. ROSCAs are becoming increasingly popular. The author lists 24 which he encountered and groups them according to characteristics. There was gender concentration in the groups. Some *arisan* were primarily social others economic. There is some consideration of Geertz's 'middle rung' thesis. The chance of improving the formal sector financial institutions could be improved by adopting some features of the informal associations.

Hospes, O. 1992. People that Count: the Forgotten Faces of Rotating Savings and Credit Associations in Indonesia, *Savings and Development*, 16 (4) pp 371-396.
The paper, originally presented at the CCCRW workshop, begins with some general criticisms about the literature and the way the issue has been treated by scholars and those interested in 'development'. The author reassesses the work of Geertz. It deals with Java, the problem of lack of written evidence, and the question of Dutch influence. It provides an authoritative summary of recent research and writing on the issue, as well as the author's own contribution.

The paper noted that Ardener limited her 1964 work. to a comparative institutional analysis. It emphasizes the need to look at the whole range of credit instruments in an area, of which the ROSCA is but one. Credit by wholesalers is very important. On the savings side it stresses that many are more concerned with the security aspect than interest rates. There is detailed work on Molucca and discussion of why ROSCAs did not evolve there at an early date. Hospes suggests that the praise given to ROSCAs in Indonesia by many needs to be interpreted with caution; analysts are fascinated by the model not the capacity of the poor to save. There are detailed footnotes and a useful bibliography.
This paper partly overlaps with (1995) Gender Differences in ROSCAs in Indonesia, in *Money-Go-Rounds: The Importance of ROSCAs for Women* (eds) S. Ardener & S. Burman. Oxford: Berg Publishers.

Hospes, O., De Groot, H. & Gerbrandy, A. 1988. NGOs Involved with Savings and Credit: (not) Making Strategic Choices? Sri Lanka: Unpublished.
The paper argues that NGOs might play an important role in mobilizing the small-scale capacities and resources of target groups, and in creating more opportunities for the poor. Chapter 2 describes the savings and borrowing behaviour of the rural poor and the range of financial intermediaries in Third World countries. It describes ROSCAs briefly, and makes a point of stressing women's roles and problems. Chapter 3 presents NGOs with several challenging issues and choices. It raises the issue whether they should be thinking of credit alone or an integrated approach. There are potential relationships between credit and savings schemes and other services, e.g. a food security system; training in skills; empowerment; advisory services, employment generation etc. The chapter looks at the conflicting loyalties often experienced by NGOs to the target group and to the need for business-like management. The fourth chapter outlines the experience of NOVIB and counterparts in savings and credit. NOVIB has been associated with 41 savings and credit programmes in Latin America (8); Africa (15) and Asia (18). Some detail is provided on these schemes. Pages 24-26 deal with ROSCAs.The last chapter concerns policy issues. There is a bibliography.

Ibe, Afarka.C. 1992 Provision of Life Insurance Services in the Informal Sector:the Case of Igbo Clubs in Ibadan, Nigeria. *Savings and Development* (Supplementary Issue) 16 (2) pp 195-202
Women's clubs are an adjunct of men's. Some clubs rotate meetings and require hosts to entertain members but few women's clubs do this.

Ibe, Afarka.C. 1990. The Structure of the Informal Credit Market in Nigeria: Lessons from Awka Town of Anambra State Ibadan *Savings and Development* 14 (4) pp 5-14.
Awka town has three banks in the area (1987) but the informal sector remains important. The author considers the informal sector as a whole and makes interesting comments on the interest rates in the sector.

Ijere, M. O. 1963. Credit Development in Nigerian Agriculture. *Nigerian Journal of Economic and Social Studies* 5 (2), 211-20.
The article gives a brief (one page) coverage of *esusu*, which is described as an improvement over the unorganized credit market.

Ikeda, R. 1918. *Actual State of Mujin and its Theories in Japanese*. Yokyo: Daisyokusha.
This work is cited in Izumida (1992).

Illy, H. F. 1973. Saving and Credit of the Bamileke in Cameroun: A Study of the Internal Financing of Development. In *Development Policy in Africa* (ed.) J. Voss. Bonn: Verlag Neue Gesellschaft, pp 293-314.
The article suggests reasons why default rates are very low.

Illy, H. F. 1978. How to Build in the Germs of Failure: Credit Cooperatives in French Cameroun. *Rural Africana* 2 (Fall), 57-67.

This article does not deal with *tontine* (ROSCAs) in any detail but it does deal with the social structure of the Banku and Bamileke peoples. The latter have a highly structured hierarchical organization where *tontine* are able to thrive. The author does not see the *tontine* as the basis for cooperative organization.

Government of India. (1991). *A Review of the Agricultural Credit System in India*. Agricultural Credit Review Committee.

Isong, G. N. 1959. *Modernization of the Esusu Credit Societies*. Nigerian Institute of Social and Economic Research, Conference Proceedings. Dec. 1959. pp. 111-129.
Not consulted.

Ito, L. S. 1952. *Ko* - Japanese Confraternities. *Monumenta Nipponica* **8**, 412-5.
This touches on *ko*.

Izumida, Y. 1992. The *Kou* in Japan: A Precursor of Modern Finance. In *Informal Finance in Low-Income Countries* (eds) D. W. Adams & D. A. Fitchett. Boulder: Westview Press, pp 165-180.
The *kou* were popular forms of financial intermediation, especially in the rural areas until the mid 1960s. Most have now disappeared. The writer suggests that they have played an important role in the formative stages of Japanese economic development and that there are lessons here for developing countries. The article discusses the *kous* and urban *mujin*. The former date back to the 12th or 13th century. There is a brief history of the development of the associations, with statistical data on farm household debt in 1911, which illustrates the importance of *kou* finance. There are statistics on the *kou* for later periods, but there is little evidence on the use made of *kou* funds. The strengths and weaknesses of the schemes is assessed, and an account given of how they contributed to the country's modern financial system. *Mujin* are described; they date from 1901 and were regularized by law in 1915. There is a good bibliography; most of the works are in Japanese.

Jain, L. C. 1929. *Indigenous Banking in India*. London: Macmillan and Company.
This is useful background material.

Janelli, R. L. & Yim, D. 1988. Interest Rates and Rationality: Rotating Credit Associations among Seoul Women. *Journal of Korean Studies*, **6**, 165-191.
Not consulted.

Jellicoe, M. R. 1968. *Indigenous Savings Associations in Eastern Africa and the Mobilization of Domestic Savings*. Economic Commission for Africa/UNESCO.
There is some data on urban societies, and Zaramo women traders involved in ROSCAs.

Jerome, T. A. 1991. The Role of Rotating Savings and Credit Associations in Mobilizing Domestic Savings in Nigeria. *Savings and Development Supplement: African Review of Money, Finance and Banking* **2**, 115-125.
The author argues that ROSCAs have been very significant despite a lot of problems, and that they have not been sufficiently appreciated. He would like to see a the role of the associations enhanced. There is some data on the groups, including the various names they are known by, the usurious interest rates, and the use of funds.

Jiggins, J. 1985. Rural Women, Money and Financial Services. *Community Development Journal* **20** (3), 163-175.
Pages 164-167 deal with ROSCAs. Savings can be made in cash or kind. Jiggins describes them as becoming increasingly commercial and less social. They can run into difficulties; and the advantages of ROSCAs have been exaggerated.

Jiggins, J. 1989. How Poor Women Earn Income in Sub-Sahara Africa and what Works against them. *World Development: Special Issue: Beyond survival:Expanding Income Earning Opportunities for Women in Developing Countries* **17** (7), 953-963.
The paper gives an overview of women's role in income generation. There is a brief section on credit and financial services, with mention of Cameroon and *tontines*.

Johnny, M. 1985. *Informal Credit for Integrated Rural Development in Sierra Leone* Hamburg: Verlag Weltarchiv GmbH.
Not consulted.

Kapferer, B. 1976. Introduction: Transactional Models Reconsidered. In *Transaction and Meaning: Directions in the Anthropology of Exchange and Symbolic Behaviour* (ed.) B. Kapferer. Philadelphia: ISHI, pp 1-27.
The book deals with a transactional perspective of social anthropology. It looks at subjective values as well as the goods that change hands in any transaction.

Katzin, M. F. 1959. 'Partners': An Informal Savings Institution in Jamaica. *Social and Economic Studies* **VIII**, 436-40.
The most important source of savings in Kingston for traders was the 'partners'. The author thinks they are of African origin. In a footnote the author refers to a communication from Bernic Kaplan about associations among the Peruvian Amerindians.

Katzin, M. F. 1959. The Jamaican Country Higgler. *Social and Economic Studies* **VIII** (4), 421-40.
Not consulted.

Katzin, M. F. 1960. The Business of Higglering in Jamaica. *Social and Economic Studies* **IX** (3), 297-331.
Not consulted.

Katzin, M. 1964. The Role of the Small Entrepreneur. In *Economic Transition in Africa* (eds) M. J. Herskovits & M. Harwitz. London: Routledge and Kegan Paul, pp 179-198.
The article deals with the informal sector and the role of the banker/money guard. It draws upon secondary material.

Kaur, M. 1990. *A Sociological Study of Rotating Credit Associations among Women.* University of Punjab.
Not consulted.

Kawashima, T. & Yozou, W. 1944. *Kou* Custom and Village Life (in Japanese). *Journal of Association of Law* **62**, 5-9.
Not consulted.

Keigo, S. n.d. Nenrei Shudan. *Nihon Minzokugaku Taikei* 3, 154-6.
There is a summary of work done on *donen-ko*, in Japan.

Kekenou, P. 1974. *Tontine et Financement des activites Economique a L'ouest du Cameroun.* Yaounde: University of Yaounde.
Not consulted.

Kelley, A. C. 1988. Population Pressures, Saving and Investment in the Third World: some puzzles. *Economic Development and Cultural Change* **36** (iii), 449-464.
There is a discussion of the impact of household size on savings, and the age-dependency effect.

Kennedy, G. F. 1973. The Korean Fiscal Kye (Rotating Credit Association). Ph. D. Diss. University of Hawaii.
Not consulted.

Kern, J. R. 1986. The Growth of Decentralized Rural Credit Institutions in Indonesia. In *Central Government and Local Development in Indonesia* (ed.) C. MacAndrews. Oxford: Oxford University Press.
The author notes the popularity of ROSCAs but regards them as inefficient mobilizers of savings and inefficient as financial intermediaries.

Kerri, J. N. 1976. Studying Voluntary Associations as Adaptive Mechanisms: A Review of Anthropological Perspectives. *Current Anthropology* **17** (1), 23-47.
Kerri outlines the contribution to the literature on voluntary associations: Anderson, Little, Banton, Geertz, Ardener and Ottenburg. He claims Ardener's paper suffers from over-simplification and lack of detail. He suggests that, in general, the methodology used in dealing with voluntary associations is weak; facts are used as illustrative detail, but one could equally well find facts to disprove the explanations given. Those working on the subject are not problem orientated.

Khatib-Chahidi, J. 1995. Gold Coins and Coffee Parties the Turkish Way in Northern Cyprus: ROSCAs Coping with Inflation. In *Money-Go-Rounds: The Importance of ROSCAs for Women* (eds) S. Ardener & S. Burman. Oxford, and Washington, USA: Berg Publishers.
The paper concerns rotating gold coin exchange activity in the Turkish Cypriot state. It outlined the history of Cyprus in terms of the various cultural forces that have been brought to bear on the island over the centuries. There are no written studies on the subject of ROSCAs in Cyprus. The paper is based on observation and personal communication. It seems that men do not belong to ROSCAs, although there is some basis for suspecting that they might have some sort of ROSCA to cater for their gambling activities. The paper describes a ROSCA where all the members were primary school teachers in their twenties or thirties. A hostess for each gathering provides refreshments. The party will probably cost about £10 sterling. Money is collected to purchase the gold coin. The custom is in keeping with other Cypriot traditions: rotating social functions; the giving of coins as presents; and the tremendous interest in money-changing. Purchase of gold coins can be a hedge against inflation which was, in 1992, about 65% p.a.

Kiernan, J. 1977. Poor and Puritan: An Attempt to View Zionism as a Collective Response to Urban Poverty. *African Studies* **36** (1), 31-41.
The study is of a group near Durban who run *stokvel* as insurance schemes. These are maintained by women. In the Zulu culture women are the chief mourners at funerals and the *stokfel* cater for funeral expenses. There is little evidence that the associations allow the accumulation of savings; they are more like welfare agencies.

Knez, E. I. n.d. *Ke* Mutual Aid Groups: Persistence and Change. 3, This is a short (4 page article) by someone based at the Smithsonian Institute. It traces the origins of the *ke* and has some useful references. In 1926 it was estimated that there were 20,000 *ke*, (classified into 300 types) in Korea. The Japanese tried to discourage the development of the *ke*. There are legal and illegal *ke*; some have specialized in banditry, gambling and resistance to taxation. After the liberation of Korea *ke* became important in financing business enterprise. *Ke* of up to 1000 members exist which operate lotteries. There are women's *ke*. These seem to be genuine rotating associations. In 1954 the UN Korean Reconstruction Agency and FAO advised that a sympathetic line should be taken towards the *ke*.

Konig, W. & Koch, M. 1990. External Financing of Microenterprises in LDCs: Lessons from Colombia. *Savings and Development* **14** (3), 233-246.
The authors see the unorganized money markets as restoring, in part, the social welfare lost because of imperfections in the formal sector.

Kokoali, C.T. 1987. *Umgaleb and the Failure of the Church? A Study in Voluntary Associations in Mbekweni Paari.* University of Cape Town.
A study of 4 types of *ungalebo* (mutual aid societies) including ROSCAs, in Mbekweni township, Paari, South Africa. Kokoali focuses on the religious aspects of such organizations which function as a new category of independent African church. An historical overview is followed by an analysis of *ungalebo* (plural *imigalelo*) in the context of the State of Emergency in 1986.

Koufopoulou, S. 1992. Women and Rotating Credit Associations: Turkey. Unpublished conference paper presented at the Centre for Cross-Cultural Research on Women, Queen Elizabeth House, Oxford.
The paper is based on research on refugees from Crete who had to move to Turkey. The community live on an island off the Turkish coast. There is a description of the women's afternoon meetings which have begun in the last three years, and which draw on the Turkish concept of a 'reception' day. Of eight circles of women studied every third woman participates in a meeting. The nucleus of the group is a family and this is gradually extended over time as more distant relatives or friends are introduced. The circle of 19 described is middle class and considered well-educated. The price of a gold coin is ascertained by telephone at the meeting then contributions are collected and the coin is purchased for the person whose turn it is to receive the 'gift'. The meeting takes the form of a coffee-drinking ceremony, with discussion, needlework, etc. The activity can be interpreted as a form of social interaction, the expression of ethnic identity, a form of social control, as well as a means of saving.

Krige, E.J. 1934. Some Social and Economic Facts Revealed in Native Family Budgets. *Race Relations* 1(6), 94-108.
Krige writes on the *mahodisana*, and notes the entertainment side of the associations.

Krishnan, V. 1959. *Indigenous Banking in South India* Bombay: The Bombay State Co-operative Union.
Not consulted.

Kropp, E., Marx, B., Pramod, B., Quinones, B. R. & Seibel, H. D. 1989. *Linking Self-Help Groups and Banks in Developing Countries.* Eschborn and Bangkok: GTZ; Apraca (Thailand).
Not consulted.

Kulp, D. H. 1925. *Country Life in South China* New York:
This source is quoted in Ardener, 1964. No publisher is named.

Kuper, H. 1960. *Indian People in Natal.* Durban: Durban University Press.
The *chita* or *chitu* associations among the Indians in Natal are said to have no social functions.

Kuper, H. & Kaplan, S. 1944. Voluntary Associations in an Urban Township. *African Studies* 3 (3), 178-186.
The study is based on a household survey of 218 units. Approximately 20% belonged to *stokvel* or *mahodisana*. The authors disagree with a number of statements by Hellman, including the one that they are primarily associated with women. They describe the organization of the *stokvel*. The *mahodisana* are larger associations.

Kurtz, D. V. 1973. The Rotating Credit Association: An Adaptation to Poverty. *Human Organization: Journal of the Society for Applied Anthropology* 32 / 23 (1), 49-58.
The author challenges Geertz's 'middle rung' theory and uses a different conceptual framework. He describes the Mexican-Americans in California and their *cundina* which are an insurance for survival.

Kurtz, D. V. & Showman, M. 1978. The Tanda: A Rotating Credit Association in Mexico. *Ethnology* **17** (i), 65-74.
The study concerns the urban ROSCA called *tanda*, which means alternative order. The associations are used for consumption and ceremonial purposes and very occasionally for educational needs. They have a very short cycle, participants are not greatly concerned about their place in the cycle and value the associations mainly for their savings function. The authors do not see them becoming a major force in economic development.

Kyokai, Z. S. G. 1971. *History of Mujin of Mutual Loans and Savings Banks* (in Japanese) Zenkoku Sogo Ginko Kyokai.
Cited in Izumida (1992).

Lacville, Robert, 1991. Warm Money, Cold Money, *The Guardian Weekly*, 23.6.1991.
The author in an article on 'The World Bank Report' comments on *tontine* (ROSCAs) in Africa, with special mention of West Africa; Cameroon and Rwanda.

Ladman, J. R. & Afcha, G. 1990. Group Lending: Why it Failed in Bolivia. *Savings and Development* **14** (4), 353-366.
The reasons for the failure of the Agricultural Bank's Small-Farmer Credit Programme's group lending scheme are examined. It was found that repayment records were more satisfactory where farmers formed their own groups and had a tradition of working together.

Lamberte, M. B. 1992. Informal Finance in the Philippines' Footwear Industry. In *Informal Finance in Low-Income Countries* (eds) D. Adams, & D. A. Fitchett. Boulder: Westview Press, pp 133-147.
There is a brief mention of ROSCAs (page 145). They are called *paluwagen*, and are found in the public sector and among low income urban groups. Some of these have formed themselves into co-operative credit unions, which are unregulated and belong to the informal sector.

Lamberte, M. B. & Balbosa, J. Z. 1988. Informal Savings and Credit Institutions in the Urban Areas: The Case of Co-operative Credit Unions..(88-06). Philippine Institute for Development Studies, Manila.
The paper notes that some ROSCAs transformed themselves into credit unions.

Lamberte, M. B. & Bunda, M. T. 1988. The Financial Markets in Low-Income Urban Communities: The Case of Sapang Palay. (88-05). Philippine Institute for Development Studies, Manila.
The survey found ROSCAs in the public sector and among low income households in urban areas.

Lein-Sheng, Y. 1952. *Money and Credit in China*. Harvard University Press.
Pages 75-78 mention ROSCAs.

Lelart, M. 1989. Tontines et Tontiniers sur les Marches Africains: Le Marche Saint-Michel de Cotonou. *African Review of Money and Banking*, The article looks at *tontines* or *Associations Rotatives d'Espargne et de Credit*, in Benin. The main characteristic of the ROSCAs for small traders is that of working as 'money guards' for clients.

Lelart M. & Gnansounou, S. 1989. ROSCAs and ROSCA members in the African Market Place: Saint Michel in Cotonau. *Savings and Development Supplementary Issue (African Review of Money, Finance and Banking* (1)) **13**, pp. 69-90.

Lemarchand, R. 1989. African Peasantries, Reciprocity and the Market. The Economy of Affection Reconsidered. *Cahiers d'etudes Africaines* **29** (1), 33-67.
Not consulted.

Levin, D. 1975. *Susu* and Investment in Trinidad (8). Central Statistical Office, Trinidad.
The paper has data on the age of participants, their class background and the use made of their funds. Blue collar workers invest more often than white collar members who have pension arrangements. The fund is known as a 'hand'.

Levine, D. 1972. *Wax and Gold: Tradition and Innovation in Ethiopian Culture* Chicago: University of Chicago Press.
Levine along with others argue that the *iqqub* originates with the Gurage people of Ethiopia.

Lewis, B. C. 1976. The Limitations of Group Action among Entrepreneurs: the Market Women of Abidjan, Ivory Coast. In *Women in Africa: Studies in Social and Economic Change* (eds) N. J. Hafkin & E. G. Bay. Stanford: Stanford University Press, pp 135-156.
This is one of the relatively few studies of women's associations. It discusses both northern and southern women's preferences for particular types of informal financial institutions. Among the northerners there were birth (*djigi*), marriage (*safina mani*) and pilgrimage associations. Among the southerners Lewis found that about one-third were or had been participating in an association. The ambulatory banker system was preferred by the market women.

Lewis, H. S. 1988. *Social Gatherings among the Shoa Oromo*. Paris: Societe Francaise pour les Etudes Ethiopiennes.
The paper provides specific examples of rotating credit associations among the Oromo ethnic group.

Liedholm, C. 1992. Small-Scale Enterprise Dynamics and the Evolving Role of Informal Finance. In *Informal Finance in Low Income Countries* (eds) D. Adams, & D. A. Fitchett. Boulder: Westview Press, pp 265-280.
The article examines the dynamics of small scale manufacturing in low income countries and the evolving role of informal finance in the process. The scope of the article is wide and data are drawn from many countries to illustrate that capital shortage is a constraint. There is a special need for working capital at particular points in the firms growth. Start-up capital is not such a problem. The author shows that although the informal sector is very responsive to needs there is a lack of integration, and gaps in provision for both short and long term funding.

Light, I. 1972. *Ethnic Enterprise in America.* Berkeley: University of California Press.
This is a major study of Korean entrepreneurship in the USA. Chapters 2-3 deal with the rotating credit associations.

Light, I. H. & Bonachiche, E. 1988. *Immigrant Entrepreneurs: Koreans in Los Angeles 1965-82.* Berkeley: University of California Press.
Chapter 10 deals with ROSCAs.

Light, I. & Deng, Z. 1995. Participation in ROSCAs within Korean Business Households in Los Angeles. In *Money-Go-Rounds: The Importance of ROSCAs for Women* (eds) S. Ardener & S. Burman. Oxford, and Washington, USA: Berg Publishers.
The paper deals with immigrant Koreans in Los Angeles. It describes immigration reception areas in the US. Koreans in Los Angeles represent 1.5% of the population. Their entrepreneurial activities range from the liquor trade, to dry cleaning, to gas stations and the wig industry. The paper raises a number of questions: if ROSCAs support entrepreneurship; whether they are competitive with banks; if their cycles are too short and if they raise enough capital. It gives some statistics on Korea from the Bank of Korea which has tracked ROSCAs and found in 1986 that 40% of Koreans were in ROSCAs (called *kye*). The paper is based on original research over a long time span in Los Angeles, and is the result of ethnographic data and the findings of a mail shot to members of the garment industry. It describes the methodology and outlines the way in which ROSCAs operate: meetings in restaurants, usually conducted by women, who manage household finance; they involve large sums and are regarded by the Koreans as illegal, although this is not technically the case, as no US law deals

with ROSCAs. It refers to law cases involving default by ROSCA members. ROSCAs do act illegally by employing interest rates that far exceed those laid down by the law. Koreans seem to value them partly because of the secrecy involved and the potential for avoiding taxation. It is not easy to obtain information on the associations, partly because the members imagine that they are viewed as 'backward'. It would seem that the money from the associations is used as working capital.

Light, I., Im, J.-K. & Deng, Z. 1990. Korean Rotating Credit Associations in Los Angeles. *Amerasia* **16**, 35-54.
Not consulted.

Lindauer, G. 1971. Formen des Landwirtschafttlichen Kredits. *Zentraljava, Zeitschrift fur Auslandische Landwirtschaft* **10** (3), 266-272.
This source is cited in Hospes (1992). Landauer writes that *arisan* is an important source of agricultural credit in Central Java.

Little, K. L. 1957. The Role of Voluntary Associations in West African Urbanization. *American Anthropologist* **59** (3), 579-596.
Little discusses ROSCAs under the heading of Friendly Societies. He describes *Nanamei Akpee* or Mutual Help Societies which provide benefits, charity, and savings functions. He writes that the Keta branch of one of these organizations had 400 members, mainly well educated women.

Little, K. 1962. Some Traditionally Bases Forms of Mutual Aid in West African Urbanization. *Ethnology* **1**, 197-211.
Little provides some statistics for mutual aid associations in Accra in 1954, and illustrates the social function of these. He has data on the Creoles in Freetown and on women's groups in Sierre Leone. There is some discussion of *esusu* (*osusu, susu, ozuzu*); he draws heavily on Bascom's work.

Little, K. L. 1965. *West African Urbanization: A Study of Voluntary Associations in Social Change*. Cambridge: Cambridge University Press.
Pages 47ff deal with ROSCAs.

Little, K. L. 1972. Voluntary Associations and Social Mobility among West African Women. *Canadian Journal of African Studies* **6** (2), 275-288.
Not consulted.

Little, K. L. 1973. *African Women in Towns. An Aspect of Africa's Social Revolution* Cambridge: Cambridge University Press.
There is some discussion of ROSCAs (p. 52). The author describes the role and activities of *Nanemei Akpee* (Society of Friends) among market women. There were branches in several towns. These societies made special gifts to members on occasions such as a birth, death, in times of sickness, following a robbery and so on. Well-to-do members might make interest-free loans to fellow members.

Logan, W. 1887. *Malabar Manual* Reprinted by the Government of Madras, 1951.
There are early references to the *chitty*.

Lukhele, A. K. 1988. *Stokvels*: Mobilizing an Alternative Economy. *Black Enterprise* **13**.
Not consulted.

Lukhele, A. K. 1990. *Stokvels in South Africa: Informal Savings Schemes by Blacks for the Black Community* Johannesburg: Amagi Books.
The author provides information on the origin of the term *stokvel* (which is of European origin) and some history of the associations, which seem to have originated from burial societies.

*Stokvel* may be rotating but many are not. He sees the forced removals of people as having a negative impact on *stokvels*. The findings of a market research organization, Markinor, are quoted. A survey was carried out in 1989 on *stokvels* in metropolitan areas. It concluded that the movement has increased since the National *Stokvel* Association of South Africa was established in 1988: 41% of *stokvels* were found to be savings clubs and 29% burial societies. Women were found to be the most active participants. Chapter 3 explores the links and overlap between shebeen (brewing parties run by women) and *stokvels*, which explains in part the police harassment of the *stokvels*. Chapters 4 and 5 deal with the different types of *stokvels*, e. g. burial, syndicate, religious, bulk buying. There is discussion of the sub-culture of the associations, their popularity with the better-off black South African and the default question. The first white *stokvel* started recently. The book deals briefly with relations with the formal sector. There is no bibliography.

Lycette, M. 1984. *Improving Women's Access to Credit in the Third World: Policy and Project Recommendations.* International Center for Research on Women.
Since the early 1970s international agencies have recognized the importance of credit as a way of expanding employment and earnings potential. The paper looks at the position of women who are disproportionately represented in the informal sector, and the problems of obtaining credit experienced by the small business sector, especially those run by women. In the discussion of the informal sector ROSCAs receive a very limited coverage. There is a bibliography.

Madge, C. 1991. *Intra-household use of income revenue and informal credit schemes in the Gambia.*
Indigenous financial organizations are dealt with (p. 17-) in this paper. Little work has been done on village informal finance. Women's access to formal credit through co-operatives is restricted. Women save through *asusu*. These seem to run for one year. Local credit arrangements are described as political as well as economic. Women may also resort to moneylenders who lend without interest, friends and family for credit. The paper discusses non-household forms of credit, and female moneylenders.

Maison, G. 1988. Credit Delivery System for Small-Scale Operators: Problems and Prospects. FAO/Ghana Workshop on Informal Financial Systems, Accra.
Maison dwells mainly on credit delivery facilities, but notes the popularity of the savings schemes such as the rotating *susu* clubs. He suggests their formal institutionalization but does not elaborate on how this might be achieved.

Manhertz, H. G. & Marston, D. 1979. Savings Behaviour in the Rural Sector: The Jamaican Experience. *Savings and Development* 3 (2), 136-147.
The paper shows that the most popular institution is the commercial bank. This is followed by the Cooperative Unions. The Partner associations, which probably date back to the days of slavery, are influential. A Household Survey carried out by the National Savings Committee showed the 'partners' to be the most widely used institution. The majority said that they planned in advance how they would use their savings, and house-building came top of the list followed by education. The writers see the commercial banks as creating underdevelopment in the rural areas.

March, K. S. & Taqqu, R. L. 1986. *Women's Informal Associations in Developing Countries: Catalysts for Change.* Boulder: Westview Press.
The book considers the impact of development programmes on women's voluntary associations in developing countries. The book covers labour, ritual and religious associations as well as credit. Pages 60-66 deal with ROSCAs, drawing on secondary data from Geertz and Ardener and later works. It assumes that there is a disproportionate number of women in ROSCAs, that few associations have the legal sanction of the societies in which they operate, and that they occur with greater frequency among the poorer sections of the population. It raises the Geertz'

thesis and summarizes Kurtz' criticism of it. Finally it discusses briefly the issue of whether the ROSCA can be a model for change.

Martin-Schiller, B. 1989. Social Networks in an Upland Javanese Village: Family and Community. *Prisma: The Indonesian Indicator* **46**, 32-44.
Not consulted.

Massengo, S. 1992. The OXFAM Tanzania Office: The Staff Rotating Savings and Credit Association. Unpublished conference paper presented at the Centre for Cross-Cultural Research on Women, Queen Elizabeth House, Oxford.
The paper on Tanzania provides a brief overview of the banking system in the country. Recent developments may give rise to more ROSCAs as village people will have less access to banks. The paper describes several self-help organizations, including one type formed to purchase veterinary products, and it also has a loan fund from which members can borrow in rotation, but borrowing is not obligatory. There is virtually no default partly because 'security groups' exist to make people pay. Massengo also refers briefly to other savings and credit groups for civil servants, and co-operatives for farmers, and gives data on a ROSCA where members are all OXFAM staff. ROSCAs are said to have no legal status.

Massing, A. 1978. Bibliography: Rural Capital Formation in West Africa. *Rural Africana* **2**, 95-115.
The emphasis is on agriculture. ROSCAs are included in the section entitled 'Agricultural Credit and Co-operatives'. There are few references.

Massing, A. & Seibel, H. D. 1974. *Traditional Organizations and Economic Development of Indigenous Cooperatives in Liberia*. New York: Praeger.
The authors found that of the 16 ethnic groups which they studied, 7 had 4 or more organizations for group saving and borrowing.

Mauri, A. 1977. A Policy to Mobilize Rural Savings in Less Developed Areas. *Savings and Development* **1**, (1) 14-25.
A speech given in 1975 at the FAO. Mauri outlined the drawbacks to commercial banks and spoke of ROSCAs in Africa and Asia. Links between the banks and the ROSCAs can lead to capital drain.

Mauri, A. 1986. Improvement of the Savings Mobilization Process through Institutional and Procedural Innovation. *Savings and Development* **14**(4).
This is the report of the Third International Symposium on the Mobilization of Personal Savings in Developing Countries. Savings (10-14 Dec. 1984).

Mayoux, L. & Anand, S. 1995. Gender Inequality, ROSCAs and Sectoral Employment Strategies in the South Indian Silk Industry. In *Money-Go-Rounds: The Importance of ROSCAs for Women* (eds) S. Ardener & S. Burman. Oxford, and Washington, USA: Berg Publishers.
The paper concerns *chit* funds in Kerala state, South India. It is based on field work with a group of low income silk reelers. Relatively few people (90) live in the village. *Chit* funds are described as illegal but are used by various social groups. People use *chit* funds to 'hide' money which is 'black' money. An agent approaches individuals and invites them to join. In the village some 90% belong to a *chit* fund. Women are getting involved and Mayoux's concern is how can these groups be strengthened.

Mbat, D. O. 1985. Savings Habit of Rural Households in Cross River State. An exploratory study. *Savings and Development* **9** (4), 469-482.
The author notes that there has, in the past, been a tendency to concentrate on urban households' savings behaviour. The paper examines the savings habits of rural households and the factors which influence them. The third section of the paper discusses the findings of primary research, involving 600 families. The research included the savings' capacity of the

rural poor. It was found that rural households spent less money on agricultural activities than their counterparts who live in urban areas, but who also farm and have to pay for labour. Rural households have multiple sources of income, but their sources of expenditure few. They have therefore a propensity to save commensurate with their environment. Many rural families who seem poor have large amounts of cash hidden in their houses. In these households it is difficult for husbands to know the financial resources of the wife and vice-versa. For most the only alternative to cash holdings are assets like buildings, land, bicycles: 50% were found to save with *ossusu*, only 0.5% saved at home and with a bank. Reasons were given for not saving with a bank (p. 479). The last section makes recommendations, calling for more research into savings behaviour.

McKee, K. 1989. Micro-level Strategies for Supporting Livelihoods, Employment, and Income Generation of Poor Women in the Third World: The Challenge of Significance. *World Development* **17** (7), 993-1006.
The paper looks at various strategies for supporting women's earning capacity — area, sector and function focused approaches and concludes that the latter two offer most hope. There is a very brief coverage of credit issues, which are described as the 'missing piece'.

Meillassoux, C. 1968. *Urbanization of an African Community: Voluntary Associations in Bamake*. Seattle: University of Washington Press.
Not consulted.

Mendez, K. 1990. Women's Access to Land as an Asset: an overview of the laws in 59 countries. In *Credit Opportunities for Women of the Developing World*. Santo Domingo: United Nations International Research and Training Institute for the Advancement of Women, pp 60-101.
The study looks at women's access to land as an asset with respect to three areas of law: inheritance, land reform, and access to credit. It also covers information on religious and traditional practices. In many countries there is more than one legal system, and religious or traditional law may be more favourable than more modern legislation. An overview is given of the legal situation in a range of countries in Africa, Asia, Europe and the Americas. Where specific information is available on credit it is included e.g. for Nigeria, Kenya, Zimbabwe, Ghana, Indonesia. This information is helpful but very brief. In all the 59 countries the law can be seen to inhibit women's ability to acquire land.

Messerschmidt, Don. 1972. Rotating Credit in Gurung Society: the *Dhikur* Associations of Tin Gaun. *The Himalayan Review* V(4) 23-35.
The author describes ROSCAs in Nepal (called *thukur* in the Gurung language). There are sections defining the *dhikur*, and describing its membership, organization and function. Children will form ROSCAs. The author thinks that the origin of the association was Tibetan.

Messerschmidt, D. A. 1973. Dhikur: Rotating Credit Associations in Nepal. In *The Himalayan Interface* (ed.) J. Fisher. Amsterdam.
This is a fuller version of the earlier paper by the same author.

Meyer, E. 1940. Kreditringe in Kamerum. *Koloniale Rundschau* **31**, 113-21.
There is a mention of *ngwa* in Bali, West Cameroon.

Miracle, M. 1971. Rotating Credit Associations in Latin America. *Caribbean Studies* **11** (3), 119-20.
This is a brief comment on the article by Norville and Wehrly. It suggests that there are ROSCAs in Guatemala.

Miracle, M. P., Miracle, D. S. & Cohen, L. 1980. Informal Savings Mobilization in Africa. *Economic Development and Cultural Change* **28** (4), 701-724.

The authors explain why the mass of Africans make no use of banking facilities. It describes fixed fund associations and rotating associations. It draws on some of the better-known literature on the topic, and personal communication with other scholars for information on areas like Zaire, Uganda, Malawi, Ethiopia and Zambia. One section draws on this literature and with the use of a quantitative table deals with the use of savings. The last part deals with mobile bankers. The authors point out some of the major gaps in the literature, for example lack of empirical data on the average returns on savings and the security of savings. They note that Ardener provides no evidence to support her assertion that association members find it easier to pay off debts in instalments than in a lump sum. There is a long bibliography on Africa.

Miyanaga, K. 1995. Economic *Kou* (ROSCAs) in Japan: A Review. In *Money-Go-Rounds: The Importance of ROSCAs for Women* (eds) S. Ardener & S. Burman. Oxford, & Providecen, USA: Berg Publishers.
A useful review of the Japanese and English literature on ROSCAs (*Kou*) operating in Japan until the 1960s.

Mubyarto, B. S., Soetrisno, L. & Isawan, B. 1987. *Survey of Self-Help Groups in Indonesia.* Jakarta: Bank of Indonesia/ Yogyakarta.
Not consulted.

Nadel, S. 1942. *Black Byzantium*. Oxford: Oxford University Press.
There is discussion about the *dashi* in central Nigeria.

Nafziger, E. W. 1977. *African Capitalism: a Study in Nigerian Entrepreneurship*. Stanford, California: Stanford University Press.
Not consulted.

Nash, M. 1964. Capital Savings and Credit in a Guatemalan and a Mexican Indian Peasant Society. In *Capital, Saving and Credit in Peasant Societies: Studies from Asia, Oceania, the Caribbean and Middle America* (ed.) R. Firth & B. Yamey. London: George Allen and Unwin.
There is a reference to ROSCAs among factory workers.

Nayar, C. P. S. 1973. *Chit Finance: An Exploratory Study on the Workings of Chit Funds*. Bombay: Vora and Co. Publishers (P) Ltd.
The work distinguishes between big and small *chitties*, and provides data on how funds are spent. Smaller funds are spent on consumption.

Nayar, C. P. S. 1986. Can a traditional Financial Technology Co-exist with Modern Financial Technologies? The Indian Experience. *Savings and Development* 10 (1), 31-58.
In this detailed study there is a history of the evolution of the *chit* fund. The various types of fund are explained — *chitty* with and without discounts; rotating lottery and auction *chitty*. The opportunity costs of using the system are discussed and malpractices covered. In the bibliography there is a useful listing of works relating to legislation.

Nayar, C. P. S. 1992. Strengths of Informal Financial Institutions: Examples from India. In *Informal Finance in Low-Income Countries* (eds) D. Adams & D. A. Fitchett. Boulder: Westview Press, pp 195-208.
The article deals with *chit* funds and their merits. Field data for Kerala and Tamil Nadu show that bad debt formed about 7% of total *chit* transactions, in this respect informal institutions are far superior to the formal ones.

Nelson, N. 1995. 'Women in Groups can Solve their Problems Together'. The Kiambu Group: A Successful Women's ROSCA in Mathare Valley, Nairobi (1971 to 1990). In *Money-Go-

*Rounds: The Importance for ROSCAs for Women* (eds) S. Ardener & S. Burman. Oxford, and Washington, USA: Berg Publishers.

The paper is based on acquaintance with the nucleus of a powerful women's group from the suburbs of Nairobi over a twenty-year period. It describes a rather unusual area in the 1970s where the gender ratio was atypical for an urban area. A Kiambu group had organized an *itega* (ROSCA) but it had only lasted in this form for about 4 years and then developed into a co-operative. The group registered as a co-operative in 1972 which expanded almost as an outer ring of the ROSCA. There were close links between the informal brewing activities of the group and their ROSCA activities; the central figures were described as 'barren' women, and all had some property. The women invested in real estate. By 1983 the ROSCA element had disappeared. The features of the ROSCA identified as important were the enforced savings element, development of organizational skills; upward social mobility; and the strong feminist rhetoric. There was probably an element of corruption and the question was posed as to why the ROSCA broke up — because of its success?

Newark, T. 1990. Financial Markets: Developments in Sub-Sahara Africa. Discussion and Recommended Proposals. Bureau for Africa.

The paper contains a section on informal markets, with reference to ROSCAs and *Tontine*. It notes that in Ghana there are 300 mobile bankers who have formed the Greater Accra *Susu* Collectors' Association and who aim to establish their own commercial bank.

Ngozi, O.-I. 1982. Developing Financial Institutions in Nigeria's Rural Areas: Some Farm household Perspectives. *Savings and Development* **6** (2), 169-193.

The work shows that borrowers in the informal market could borrow quite substantial sums from different loan sources. Many were lenders as well as borrowers. There is a short section on ROSCAs in the article. Of a total sample of 73 over 20% were found to be members of ROSCAs.

Nguyen, v. V. 1949. *Savings and Mutual Lending Societies (ho)*. Yale University, South East Asia Studies.

Apparently all the professional managers of the *ho* are women.

Niger-Thomas, M. 1995. Women's Access to and the Control of Credit through ROSCAs in Cameroon: The Mamfe Case. In *Money-Go-Rounds: The Importance of ROSCAs for Women* (eds) S. Ardener & S. Burman. Oxford, & Washington, USA: Berg Publishers.

The paper deals with the forest area. It gives some background on the ROSCA. Women are now showing an interest in getting in on 'big venture' business previously the domain of men. It suggests that there might be a bigger role for ROSCAs as banks begin to pull out of some areas. Of a sample of 120 women interviewed 95% belonged to a *njangi*. There are various types of associations — the 'disproportionate' *njangi*, where contributions of members may vary in volume; and ones in which the aim is to buy particular products (e.g. soap) or consumer durables (e.g. kitchen equipment). There is a description of the length of cycles, and the selling of the 'turn', drawing lots and the use of bribes. ROSCAs are central to women's interests.

Nikoi, G. 1990. Women's Access to Credit in Africa. In *Women and Credit* (ed.) Santo Domingo: INSTRAW, pp 142-161.

The study looks at Ghana. It discusses successful informal credit schemes and two formal ones which aim to improve women's access to credit. It notes that in the urban informal sector the most important institutions are the indigenous savings associations, *susu* groups which are common among the market women, but also among professional groups. The groups comprising illiterate women are, in the main, organized by men. One of the recommendations of the study is that fuller recognition should be made of the self-help financial associations

Norvell, D. J. & Wehrly, J. S. 1969. A Rotating Credit Association in the Dominican Republic. *Caribbean Studies* **9** (1), 45-52.

ROSCAs are called *san* in the Dominican Republic. In the Bahamas they are known as *esu*; in Trinidad *susu*; and in Brazil *consorcio*.. In the Dominican Republic the leader or organizer receives remuneration. The money is often used for working capital. The societies are most popular among low income groups. The authors state that they are based on authoritarian personal relationships.

Notteboom, C. 1944. Assistance Economique Mutuelle Systematisee dans L'Asia du Sud et de L'Este. *Orientalia Nederlandia*, 243-30.
Not consulted.

Nwabughuogu, A. I. 1984. The *isusu*: An Institution for Capital Formation among the Ngwa Ibo; Its Origins and Development to 1951. *Africa* **54** (4), 46-58.
The author used archival sources along with others, and gives an historical account of the rise of the ROSCAs and their bargaining strength with the colonial government. He traces the origins to the need of young men to raise a bridewealth and describes the sanctions used against defaulters. He explains how increasingly exploitative features entered the system and how leaders of the groups were able to resist proposed new colonial legislation in the 1940s.

Nwabughuogu, A. I. n.d. Indigenous Thrift and Credit versus Modern Thrift and Credit Societies in Southeastern Nigeria 1936-51. *Journal of the Historical Society of Sierre Leone*.
Not consulted.

Nzemen, M. 1988. *Theorie de la Practique des Tontines au Cameroun* Yaounde: Societe de Presse et d' Editions du Cameroun.
Not consulted.

Odozi, C. M. 1983. *Financial Intermediaries in the Nigerian Economy. The Role of the Rotating Credit System in the Economic Development of Bendel State*. University of Benin.
Not consulted.

Ohio State University. 1989. *Annotated Bibliography on Agricultural Credit and Rural Savings XIII*: A Special Issue on Informal Finance. Columbus, Ohio State University.

Okediji, O. O. 1975. On Voluntary Associations as an Adaptive Mechanism in West African Urbanization: Another Perspective. *African Urban Notes* **B** (2), 51-73.
Not consulted.

Okeyo, A. P. 1979. Women in the Household Economy: Managing Multiple Roles. *Studies in Family Planning; Special Issue — Learning about Rural Women* **10** (11/12).
Not consulted.

Okonjo, K. 1977. Financial Institutions and the Mobilization of Resources for Investment and Consumption in the Rural Areas: Women and *Esusu* in Two Western Igbo Communities. In *African Women by African Women of Africa* (eds) G. Awe & F. Steady. New York.

Okonjo, K. 1979. Rural Women's Credit Systems: A Nigerian Example. *Studies in Family Planning* **10** (11/12), 326-331.
The article concerns two towns in Bendel state. The clubs are known as *esusu* , *otu-otu* and *otu-ofu*. It seems that women dominate them. The money from the clubs is used as start-up capital and as a safety net in hard times. In a sample of 200 it was found that 90% belonged to at least one club. Those who did not belong to a club were the young (under 18 years). Women used the savings from the clubs for investment in cloth manufacture, education, and drinking bars. They did not use it to buy land, or for farming activities. In one of the towns which had a woman as a leader the women were encouraged to improve the market place investing their money in more substantial shelters.

Okorie, F. A. & Miller, L. F. 1976. *Esusu* Clubs and their Performance in Mobilizing Rural Savings and Extending Credit: Ohaozara Sub-division, East Central State, Nigeria (AETR/76.1). University of Ibadan, Department of Agricultural Economics.
Not consulted.

Olivier, M. 1990. Credit Opportunities for Women of the Developing World. In *Women and Credit*. Santo Domingo: United Nations International Research and Training Institute for the Advancement of Women, pp 20-59.
The article focuses on the need to improve women's capital resources in order to increase their employment and productivity. It examines a number of successful credit programmes for low-income women, and draws lessons from these. It discusses the policy implications of subsidized credit.

Oludimu, O. L. & Fabiyi, Y. L. 1983. The Mobilization of Credit *Savings and Development* 7 (4), 379-393.

Oludimu, O. L. & Fabiyi, Y. L. 1984. Providing and Utilizing Credit for Agricultural Development in Nigeria: a case study of the Cross River State. *Savings and Development* 8 (2), 175-187.
The paper looks at the effectiveness of credit administration from the perspective of the farmer and the loan agency. It includes a literature review on the subject, and draws upon research carried out in 1981 in 7 areas. The work does not deal with ROSCAs as such but throws some light upon rural borrowers' preferences for the source of loans and challenges some popular assumptions. The research showed that contrary to popular belief farmers were of aware of the credit facilities available; 78 out of 102 were actually pursuing loans, and that formal sources of credit were used more than informal ones — 33 as opposed to 7. The article has some interesting data on why some respondents preferred informal sources. These were usually small borrowers who felt that the informal sector provided more flexible services, less complex administrative procedures, and a close relationship of trust between borrower and creditor.

Oludimu, O. 1989. The Political Economy of Rural Savings Mobilization. *Scandanavian Journal of Development Alternatives* VIII (4), 139-146.
This is a broad overview of the issues with stress on the paramount importance of domestic savings.

Ong, M. L., Adams, D. W. & Singh, I. (n.d.). Voluntary Rural Savings Capacity in Taiwan. Ohio State University, Department of Agricultural Economics and Rural Sociology.
Not consulted.

Osuntogun, A. & Adeyemo, R. 1981. Mobilization of Rural Savings and Credit Expansion by Pre-Cooperative Organizations in South Western Nigeria. *Savings and Development* 5 (4), 247-260.
The ROSCAs are seen as pre-cooperative organizations, catering for men, women and some children of all social classes; in open societies membership cuts across occupational groups. There are brief references to other African countries. The article is based on research carried out in 1979-80, and covered 59 societies. The characteristics of ROSCAs are given briefly: in this area the officers are paid, and women are not very prominent. In 19 societies there were no female members and even in other mixed societies they were in the minority and were poorly represented on committees. The article describes admission procedures, sanctions, value of savings and loan terms and interest rates: 53% granted loans to members but few were able to secure external loans against their their savings: 80% attempted to but only 5 were successful. There are statistical tables comparing the 3 states, and detailing the use of funds. The main reason given by members for joining a ROSCA was to obtain credit. The author notes the flexibility of the organizations; their role in fostering community solidarity, tradition and yet accommodating change.

Otero, M. & Downing, J. 1989. Meeting Women's Financial Needs: Lessons for Formal Financial Institutions (12). Ohio State University.
This paper was prepared for a conference sponsored by the World Bank, USAID, and Ohio State University. It suggests that women farmers need longer term loans than are currently provided by the informal sector. Its recommendations are that there should not be subsidized credit. Loans must reflect the commercial rates or be higher; in this way the capacity of the poor to save and borrow will be vindicated and the aid programmes will be able to cover their costs and generate income. It refers to ACCION's work in Latin America to link the informal and the formal, and Ohio State University research on Zaire and Niger.

Ottenberg, S. 1959. Improvement Associations among the Afikpo Ibo. *Africa* **25** (1), 1-23.
Not consulted.

Ottenberg, S. 1968. The Development of Credit Associations in the Changing Economy of the Afikpo Igbo. *Africa* **38** (3), 237-252.
This is a study of an area in Eastern Nigeria of 22 villages. The fieldwork was carried out in 1951-53 and 1959-60. It has no detailed economic data, but it raises some interesting questions as to where loan associations arose and why. There are suggestions for the causes of the constraints on women. In general the writer takes the same line as Geertz. He seeks to explain, in structural terms, the emergence of the groups in some societies and not others.

Owualah, S. I. 1984. Competition for Bank Deposits in Nigeria. *Savings and Development* **8** (2), 159-172.
The article reviews the policy to stimulate savings mobilization in Nigeria. It notes that, among the poor, the commercial banks have been mainly interested in savings accounts.

Padmanabhan, K. P. 1988. *Rural Credit: Lessons for Rural Bankers and Policy Makers*. London: IT Publications.
In a section on the linking of informal savings clubs with other financial institutions the author provides some material on Ethiopia where the *ikub* is extremely popular. Membership is said to include 60% of the population in the period 1963-73 8-10% of GDP was estimated to have been saved through *ikubs*.

Pananek, H. & Schwede, L. 1988. Women are Good with Money: Earning and Managing in an Indonesian City. In *A Home Divided: Women and Income in the Third World* (eds) D. Dwyer & J. Bruce. Stanford: Stanford University Press, pp 71-98.
The study, conducted in the early 1970s, found widespread use of *arisan* by middle class and lower middle class women in Jakata.

Pankhurst & Eshete, E. 1958. Self-help in Ethiopia. *Ethiopian Observer* **2** (1).
This traces the origins of the *iqqub*. It is mentioned in D. Aredo above.

Partadireja, A. 1974. Rural Credit: the Ijon System. *Bulletin of Indonesian Economic Studies* **10**, 54-71.
Not consulted.

Phillips, R.E. (n.d.) The Bantu in the City: *A Study of Cultural Adjustment on the Witwatersrand*. South Africa, Lovedale Press.
The work is cited in Elmar Thomas below.

Pische, J. D. von, 1975. A Penny Saved: Kenya's Cooperative Savings Scheme and Some Related Aspects of Rural Finance. Institute of Development Studies, Nairobi.
Not consulted.

Pischke, J. D. von, 1991. *Finance at the Frontier: Debt Capacity and the Role of Credit in the Private Economy*. The World Bank.

There are some references to ROSCAs on pages 13-17, 50, 217; 306.

Pischke, J. D. von, 1992. ROSCAs: State-of-the-Art Financial Intermediation. In *Informal Finance in Low-Income Countries* (eds) D. W. Adams & D. A. Fitchett. Boulder: Westview Press, pp 325-335.
The author writes that experience has shown that direct intervention to displace informal finance, to limit its alleged abuses, or to overcome its presumed shortcomings has a pathology of its own. First it is a costly failure. There is a discussion of the ROSCA, which is described as the most important model for working from the informal to the formal. The reasons for this are that it is widespread, that it does intermediate, that it is popular and appropriate to its cultural context. The author highlights the strengths of the associations and describes them as having a winning formula.

Pischke, J. D.von & Rouse, J. 1983. Selected Successful Experiences in Agricultural Credit and Rural Finance in Africa. *Savings and Development* **7** (1), 21-37.
The author gives an overview of institutional credit performance in rural Africa and gives 6 examples of partial success in providing loans to farmers. In general, however, the picture is disappointing and the evidence is not very clear as to whether loans have increased the pool of funds available for the rural sector or merely substituted existing sources. One section deals with ROSCAs, describing their essential characteristics. There is a concise summary of the positive features of the associations, and theories put forward concerning the use of funds, and ways in which they are adapting to modern needs. The author concludes that ROSCA diversity prevents specific conclusions but that generalizations may be suggested. These are that there is a demand for financial institutions even among the poor that this reflects certain levels of liquidity; and that certain traditional modes of interaction support appropriate financial intermediation for the participants.

Plaut, S. 1985. The Theory of Collateral. *Journal of Banking and Finance* **9**, 401-419.
Not consulted.

Putnam, Robert D., Leonardi, Robert & Nanetti, Raffaella, 1992. *Governance and the Civic Community: Social Capital and Institutional Success in Italy's Regions*, N. J. Princeton University Press.
A section of chapter 6 has some discussion of ROSCAs, and draws on the work of a number of leading writers on the subject (Ardener, Geertz, Velez-Ibanez).

Quarcoo, P. K. 1980. Strategies for Unifying Domestic Capital Markets in LDCs. *Savings and Development* **4** (2), 139-154.
There is a short section on informal groups on pages 149-50. It mentions the role of informal sanctions and local knowledge about credit-worthiness. Informal groups may increase the political influence of small entrepreneurs.

Rahmato, D. 1991. Investing in Tradition: Peasant and Rural Institutions in Post-Revolutionary Ethiopia. *Sociologia Ruralis* **XXXI** (2/3), 169-183.
The article is based on field work 1989-90. It is concerned with rural support groups in general, particularly with the welfare elements. The *amba* are credit service clubs. The article is of interest in that it shows that animals etc., provided as forms of assistance by NGOs, were often sold off to cover burial expenses and household consumption.

Rhadhakrishnan, S. *et al.* 1975. *Chit Funds*. Madras: Institute for Financial Management and Research.
Not consulted.

Robertson, C. 1982. Ga Women and Socio-Economic Change in Accra, Ghana. In *Women in Africa: Studies in Social and Economic Change*. (eds) N. J. Hafkin & E. G. Bay. Stanford: Stanford University Press, pp 111-133.

The author says that the ROSCAs are of recent origin, probably post 1945. The first references to *susu* in records are from this date. The associations were found to be becoming increasingly popular.

Ross, F. 1990. Strategies Against Patriarchy: Women and Rotating Credit Associations. B.Sc. Hons. Thesis, University of Cape Town.
Female participation of the two core ROSCAs is analysed in the Cape Town area. Economic motivation and perceived options are discussed in an attempt to understand the social meanings of ROSCAs in the context of the 'triple oppression' of black South African women. ROSCAs enable women to achieve social and economic independence within the broader framework of a very patriarchal society, although female membership is not necessarily articulated in these terms.

Rouchy, J.-Y. 1983. Un Mecanisme d'Accumulation et de Couverture Sociale Specifique: les Tontines. *Etudes pour le Development* **2**, 121-127.
Not consulted.

Rowlands, M. 1995. Looking at Financial Landscapes: A Contextual Analysis of ROSCAs in Cameroon. In *Money-Go-Rounds: The Importance of ROSCAs for Women* (eds) S. Ardener & S. Burman. Oxford, and Washington, USA: Berg Publishers.
The paper draws on work on entrepreneurship in the Cameroon. The introduction covers the government's work in the 1980s to support entrepreneurs as a means to achieving economic revival in the country. This involved creating a new national bourgeoisie. There was antipathy to the Bamileke and the Anglophone businessmen who were seen as 'traitors' and old style operators. The section on ROSCAs draws on interview material with 30 businessmen and on the work of French anthropologists. Cameroon businessmen have established successful south-south links and use aid agencies to get the technical aid which they need. The paper points to a danger of polarization of the economy. There are two types of *tontine* — one is a mutual aid type, relatively small in money terms, sometimes called *njangi*, and found everywhere; the other is the business ROSCA, which involves larger sums, uses an auction system, and where contributions may vary from month to month. Membership of the two types is distinct, although individuals may belong to both. Rowlands lists the advantages of ROSCAs — rapidity of access to funds, mutual support, stress on saving, but also the disadvantages — need for projects with quick returns; tendency to diversification, and taking the short term view with its negative impact on management. The limits to ROSCAs can be seen in terms of scale and the short term nature of the cycles; there is an urgent need for diversification. They are not a substitute for a banking system.

Ruel, M. 1969. The Modern Adaptation of Associations of the Banyang of the West Cameroon. *Southwestern Journal of Anthropology* **20**, 1-41.
Not consulted.

Rustam, K. S. 1986. Grass-root Development with PKK. *Prisma: The Indonesian Indicator* **40**, 77-84.
Cited in Hospes (1992). The government has clearly played a major role in stimulating the development of ROSCAs and has used them as a vehicle for some of its social welfare programmes, notably in health and housing.

Sanderatne, N. 1992. Informal Finance in Sri Lanka. In *Informal Finance in Low-Income Countries* (eds) D. Adams & D. A. Fitchett. Boulder: Westview Press, pp 85-101.
This paper does not deal with ROSCAs in any detail but mentions *cheetus*, and says that they are widespread. There is a section of the paper on linking the formal and informal sectors, some experiments have been made in this direction. One recommendation involves NGOs. The major recommendation is for an increase in the number of lending institutions.

Sanneh, S. M. 1975. Rotating Credit Associations and their Potential in the Agricultural Development of Ghana. Madison, University of Wisconsin.
Not consulted.

Scheepens, T. J. 1974. Socio-economic Research about Traditional Savings and Credit Organizations in Comparison with Modern Organizations in Desa Bojong, Jawa Barat, Indonesia. Wageningen Agricultural University, The Netherlands.
This work is cited in Hospes (1992).

Schildkrout, E. 1982. Dependence and Autonomy: the Economic Activities of Secluded Hausa Women in Kano, Nigeria. In *Women and Work in Africa* (ed.) E. G. Bay. Boulder: Westview Press, pp 55-61.
The article looks at the various ways in which Hausa women are able to earn money. Membership of a ROSCA is a way of capital formation.

Schmidt, R. H. & Kropp, E. 1987. *Rural Finance: Guiding Principles*. Eschborn: GTZ and DSE.
There is discussion of informal finance, but very little comment on ROSCAs, except to say that there is minimal risk of officials abusing power in a ROSCA. The author suggests that the existence of self-help groups is an instrument against the government, the formal sector and the financial environment. He stresses the importance of knowledge of the role, scope and practices of the informal sector and the possibility of strengthening links between the formal and informal.

Schrader, H. 1991. Rotating Credit Associations: Institutions in the 'Middle Rung' of Development? Working Paper 148. Sociology of Development Research Centre, Bielefeld.
This paper is cited in Hospes (1992) and listed in Schrader (1992) below.

Schrader, H. 1992. The Socio-economic Functions of Money Lenders in Expanding Economies; the case of the Chettiers. *Savings and Development* 16 (1) pp 69-82.
The article considers the role of chettiers in the British colonial system in India, Burma, Malaya and Ceylon. There is reference to ROSCAs (p. 78) in the section on contemporary part time money lenders and some consideration of Geertz's thesis.

Schwartz, A. 1969. Solidarity Clanique, Integration Urbaine et Chamage en Afrique Noire. *Journal Canadien des Etudes Africanes* 3 (2), 393.
Not consulted.

Seibel, H. D. 1985. Saving for Development: a Linkage Model for Informal and Formal Financial Markets. *Quarterly Journal of International Agriculture (Germany)* 24, 390-98.
This paper was given at a UN symposium on the Mobilization of Personal Savings In Developing Countries (Yaounde, 1984).

Seibel, H. D. & Marx, M. T. 1987. *Dual Financial Markets in Africa: Case Studies of Linkages Between Informal and Formal Financial Institutions*. Saarbruecken/Fort Lauderdale: Breitenbach Publishers.
The authors cast doubt upon the ability of ROSCAs to act as agents for development. They suggest that if they were upgraded into permanent savings and loan institutions they would be more effective.

Seibel, H. D. 1989. *Finance with the Poor, by the Poor. Financial Technologies for the Informal Sector Social Strategies*. Forschungsberichte 3/2 December 1989.
Not consulted.

Seibel, H. D. & Parhusip, U. 1992. Linking Formal and Informal Finance: the Indonesian Example. In *Informal finance in Low-Income Countries*. (eds) D. W. Adams & D. A. Fitchett. Boulder: Westview Press, pp 239-248.

The article argues that linking self-help groups more closely with the formal sector can solve the transaction cost problem. The report covers an experiment in Indonesia to enhance the links between the formal and informal sectors. Trials had taken place in Cameroun and Nigeria by a German agency, and focused especially on ROSCAs. The Asian and Pacific Regional Agricultural Credit Association, with the German agency's (GTZ) assistance decided to try the same policy in Thailand, Philippines, Nepal and Indonesia. The pilot began in 1988. It was found that in Indonesia because of the enormous diversity of conditions no single model was appropriate. Members of self-help group were trained and the banks were involved in the scheme, group loans were made. About 50% of those involved were women. Most savings clubs associated with the scheme have been able to increase their savings. The authors consider it to be too early to judge the sustainability of the scheme but they are optimistic.

Seibel, H. D. & Shrestha, B. P. 1988. Dhikuti: The Small Businessman's Informal Self-help Bank in Nepal. *Savings and Development* 12 (2), 183-198.

The article focuses on ROSCAs. It suggests that there have been 4 main trends in their development with the growth of monetization and a market economy, and illustrates this with reference to Nepal. It describes the development of the *dhikuti* among the Thakali people. The associations have become the major source of non-farm credit in the country. A striking feature was the rotation period of 25-30 years in the 1960s. The article draws heavily on the work of Messerschnidt (1972) for detail of ROSCAs among other ethnic groups in Nepal. There is detail on contributions, monthly cycles, bidding, and incremental payments (interest equivalents). The value of linking the associations with banks and the drawbacks of the institutions as observed by participants themselves is discussed.

Sethi, R. M. 1995. Women's ROSCAs: Their Relevance in Contemporary Indian Society. In *Money-Go-Rounds: The Importance of ROSCAs for Women* (eds) S. Ardener & S. Burman. Oxford, and Washington, USA: Berg Publishers.

The paper shows that ROSCAs — *chit* funds - are widespread in India but that they have a much longer history in the south. Rotating schemes have been popular since the 1950s in northern India, but there is a dearth of literature on them. There is an historical perspective to the *chit* funds, with possible explanations as to their origin; documentary evidence of their existence on the Malabar coast in the 19th century; their spread north in the mid 20th century and government legislation to regulate the *chit* funds. There are details of the legislation of various states and reference to the Central Bank Committee Report of 1921 on the informal financial organizations and description of three types of rotating arrangements. The paper is detailed on types of schemes and legislation. The functions of ROSCAs are seen to be accumulation of savings; social solidarity. Some clubs have a degree of exclusivity. Some are popular with housewives, some provide seed money for the garment trade, garden nurseries and boutiques. The role of kinsmen is becoming increasingly ambivalent in India and and to some extent the ROSCA fills this role.

Sexton, L. D. 1982. Customary and Corporative Models for Women's Development Organizations (41). IASER, Port Moresbury.

The paper describes an interest free credit system in operation between groups; loans are made in cash. These are not ROSCAs but *wok meri*. There is a reference to ROSCAs.

Sexton, L. D. 1982b. *Wok Meri*: A Women's Savings and Exchange System in Highland Papua, New Guinea. *Oceania* 52, 167-198.

The article describes newly-formed women's self-help groups, which have economic and social functions and are modelled on male associations. The women have received support from men for some of their activities, but ridicule and even violent reaction to others. They have managed to establish women's courts to deal with male offenders.

Shanmugam, B. 1989. Development Strategy and Mobilizing Savings through ROSCAs: The Case of Malaysia. *Savings and Development* **13** (4), 351-367.
ROSCAs have become more widespread in the last 5-10 years. They are more popular among the Malays and Indians than among the more affluent Chinese. The paper describes 3 types and explains their popularity. They are forbidden by law under the Kootu Funds (Prohibition) Act 1971. The author suggests that there are policy implications to be learned for government and the formal sector. He discusses the economic significance of ROSCAs.

Shanmugan, B. 1988a. Tontine Operations in Malaysia. *Asian Profile* Oct.

Shanmugan, B. 1991. Socio-economic Development through the Informal Credit Market. *Modern Asian Studies* **25** (4), 209-225.
There is some discussion of the widespread existence of the ROSCAs throughout the world and especially in Asia. It is probable that the Indians brought the idea of ROSCAs to Malaya. The author thinks that ROSCAs for consumer durables is unique to Malaya. He describes housewives and maids forming groups to 'win' consumer durables. Another form of ROSCA found is the discounting one where members may bid for the funds. This type is very popular and ROSCAs generally have become much more numerous in the last five to ten years.

Skeldon, R. 1980. Regional Associations among Urban Migrants in Papua New Guinea. *Oceania* **50**, 248-272.
The article has an introduction about voluntary associations in general, but concentrates on regional associations. In Papua New Guinea these are not highly developed; the most common are football associations. There are case studies which show the importance of the welfare aspects of the groups. ROSCAs of the highlanders are called *Lae*, or *Sundaying*. Some associations develop into pressure groups.

Slover, C. H. 1991. The Effect of Membership Homogeneity on Group Size, Funds Mobilization, and the Engenderment of Reciprocal Obligations among Informal Financial Groups in Rural Zaire. Paper presented at the Seminar on Finance and Rural Development in West Africa, OSU/CIRAD, October 21-25.
Not consulted.

Smith, A. H. 1899. *Village Life in China*. New York: Revell.
Smith describes ROSCAs in China in the late nineteenth century. Groups were small and meetings regular but infrequent. As described by Smith they appear to have been rather vulnerable to economic shocks. Pages 152-60 are relevant.

Smith, D. H. & Phillheimer, K. 1983. Self-Help Groups as Social Movement Organizations: Social Structure and Social Change. *Research in Social Movements Conflicts and Change* **5**, 203-233.
Not consulted.

Smith, R. J. & Wiswell, E. L. 1982. *The Women of Suye Mura*. Chicago: University of Chicago Press.
This work is based on the detailed field notes of Embree's widow. Pages 38-62 are relevant.

Smith, R. T. 1964. Ethnic Differences and Peasant Economy in British Guiana. In *Capital, Saving and Credit in Peasant Societies* (eds) R. Firth & B. Yamey. London: George Allen and Unwin, pp 305-329.
The author writes that one of the most usual forms individual savings is the *box* by hand holders. Money accumulated in this way is usually spent on consumer goods. The treatment of the subject is very brief.

Soen, D. & De Comarmond, P. 1971. Savings Associations among the Bamilèkè. Traditional and Modern Co-operation in South West Cameroon. *Journal de la Société des Africanistes* **XLI** (2), 189-201, and *American Anthropologist* **74**, 1170-1179.
The authors note evidence of nepotism and corruption. They found urban and rural associations to be very similar. Various market economy elements had been introduced into the traditional societies, for example the notion of interest, deposits, etc.

Srinivasan, S. 1995. A Note on ROSCAs among South Asians in Oxford. In *Money-Go-Rounds: The Importance of ROSCAs for Women* (eds) S. Ardener & S. Burman. Oxford, and Washington, USA: Berg Publishers.
The paper is based on research on Indians in Oxford among two distinct communities, one from the north — Punjabi speaking; and one from the south, mainly from the Kerala area. It gives some statistical data on the numbers of immigrants from these areas in Oxford and their occupations. The survey was of 94 enterprises. All are small businesses or restaurants. The northerners are the more entrepreneurial group. The research showed that none had relied on ROSCAs for start-up capital, but had taken out bank loans. ROSCAs are seen to be for women. ROSCAs were, however, important in the 1960s when the first Asian shops began to open. ROSCA money has been important for house purchase according to work by Shore. Srinivasan found it was still important in East Oxford, and was mainly a female activity. She describes a committee of the northern group 'cutting the *chit*', and lists the purposes to which savings are put — marriages, school fees, trips to India. There is little social dimension to these clubs. The southerners' systems are slightly different, men being more actively involved, but the main point of interest is the use put to the funds. Deposits are frequently made in Indian banks in sterling deposit accounts which earn high interest and are tax free, they also invest in property in Kerala. UK banks are not attractive to this group, they prefer greater secrecy about their savings.

Stiglitz, J. E. & Weiss, A. 1981. Credit Rationing in Markets with Imperfect Information. *American Economic Review* **LXXI** (June), 393-410.
Viewed by economists as a seminal article on the role of information in credit markets.

Stockhausen, J. von. 1982. Credit Groups and Rotating Savings and Credit Associations - Different Financial Technologies? *Quarterly Journal of International Agriculture (Germany)* **21**, 115-72.
Not consulted.

Stockhausen, J. von 1988. *Credit Guarantee Schemes for Small Farmers*. ifo.
The work has a short consideration of grass-roots organizations (pp 40-49, 63), and the FAO Program of People's Participation (PPP). There is a brief discussion of the role of self-help groups as intermediaries between the banking sector and individual small entrepreneurs, with reference to the Saemaul organizations in South Korea. These have been set up to complement the co-operatives and owe much to the model of the ROSCA. There is mention of the *Saemaul* Women's Clubs where there is a rice savings campaign. There is a useful bibliography.

Strathern, M. 1975. *No Money on Our Skins: Hagen Migrants in Port Moresby*. Port Moresby: New Guinea Research Bulletin.
This is a lengthy study of migration among a relatively small ethnic group to Port Moresby. Chapter 7 looks at the business issues of the Hagen migrants. Much money is used to maintain an urban life-style, and to keep up social relationships. Spending is said to fall into two types, one of which is credit schemes — *mekim sande* (make Sunday), or *kampani* (in alliance). People who receive payment on the same day form small groups, often of between 2-4 persons. They make contributions of 60-70% of their earnings to the pool fund which is picked up by one member. This is viewed mainly as a form of saving, but also has an important form of social investment, cementing friendships. In the *kampani*, at least, non-Hageners are often included. The evidence from a small survey indicated that it was younger single men who

tended to belong to the *sande* as they had more disposable income. The study looked at the uses to which money taken from the ROSCA was put.

Subbarama, A. 1925. *Economic Life in a Malabar Village.* Bangalore: The Bangalore Printing and Publishing Co. Ltd.
Not consulted.

Summerfield, H. 1995. A Note on ROSCAs among Northern Somali Women in the UK. In *Money-Go-Rounds: The Importance of ROSCAs for Women* (eds) S. Ardener & S. Burman. Oxford, and Washington, USA: Berg Publishers.
This is a study of Somali women in London.

Swift, M. G. 1964. Capital, Saving and Credit in an Malay Peasant Economy. In *Capital, Saving and Credit in Peasant Societies.* (eds) R. Firth & B. Yamey. London: George Allen and Unwin, pp 133-156.
The article mentions ROSCAs briefly (p. 140). He describes temporary loan associations called *kutu*. He writes that the peasant has difficulty in getting members to join because the schemes usually break down. The *kutu* are seen as socially interesting but not of great economic significance.

Symons, E. & White, J. 1984. *Banking Law.*
Mentioned by Besley, Coate and Loury (1990). Many US savings and loans institutions seem to have started as ROSCAs.

Szabo, S. 1992. Rotating Credit Associations: Lessons for Development Strategy. Centre for Cross-Cultural Research on Women, Queen Elizabeth House, Oxford, unpublished.
The paper, presented at the Centre for Cross-Cultural Research on Women workshop, looks at ROSCAs as a development strategy. It begins with an overview of women in informal markets and the marginalization of women; the advantages of ROSCAs and why they are numerous, stressing their value as a financial service — informal screening, etc. Women appear to withdraw voluntarily from banking services. The importance of targeted savings and women's control of income is covered. Savings should be viewed as an invisible good, which is fungible. Ceremonial expenditure can be viewed as a social necessity; reputation as a form of collateral. Areas for research are suggested such as the importance of regional factors, resource fungibility, opportunity costs. The paper deals very briefly with the situation in El Salvador where Szabo worked on the informal sector and micro-enterprises. A programme is operational among refugees, run by Save the Children, based upon an ILO study. The conclusions to the paper are that micro-enterprise credit programmes may replace bad moneylenders, but there is little need for development agencies to try to replace the ROSCA. Indeed it would lead to dependence, lack of input from the local people, paternalism, raised opportunity costs, and would probably disadvantage women. Any appropriate changes introduced would have to be minor, and over a very long time span.

Tebbut, Melanie. 1983. *Making Ends: Pawnbroking and Working Class Credit.* London, Methuen
There are some references to ROSCAs (*diddlums* and *knick-knack* clubs) in the north of England.

Thomas, E. 1989. Rotating Credit Associations in Cape Town: A View from Anthropology. Preliminary Report to the Small Business Development Corporation.
Not consulted.

Thomas, E. 1989. Rotating Credit Associations in Cape Town. Paper presented at the Annual Conference of the Association for Anthropologists in Southern Africa, University of Western Cape, 13-16 September.

The author mentions Ardener's work and Geertz, but says there is little literature on ROSCAs. He gives a brief history of the associations in South Africa drawing on secondary sources. He provides a brief literature review relevant to the area. The earliest references seem to date from the 1930s (Hellman) and it seems that women dominated the associations. He describes fieldwork (Nov. 1988-May 1989) during which time he was able to interview members of 15 associations in the Cape Town area. He describes three types of ROSCA; all had officials to take care of records, etc. The small-scale *gooi-goois* are essentially savings clubs and they usually last about 6 months of the year. The sale of 'shares' is possible. Investment clubs are not real ROSCAs, in the form defined by Ardener, but members see them as falling into the same generic category. High budget associations are those with 100 members of more, and where there is a hierarchical structure with great power lying with the officials. These are described in some detail. The author describes the ROSCAs taking legal action against defaulters on occasion. ROSCAs are growing in number and attracting the attention of financial institutions in the formal sector.

Timberg, T. A. & Aiyar, C. V. 1984. Informal Credit Markets in India. *Economic Development and Cultural Change* **33** (1), 43-59.
This is one of the earliest studies of urban informal markets. It deals with indigenous bankers, the scale of their operations, interest rates, etc.

Tokutaro, S. 1962. *Koshudan Seiritsu Katei no Kenkyu*. Tokyo: Yoshikawa Kobunkan.
There is a passing reference to the *ko*.

Topley, M. 1964. Capital, Saving and Credit among Indigenous Rice Farmers and Immigrant Vegetable Farmers in Hong Kong's New Territories. In *Capital, Saving and Credit in Peasant Societies* (eds) R. Firth & B. Yamey. London: George Allen and Unwin, pp 157-186.
Pages 177-178 deal with traditional associations which are described as purely credit associations. Some save for a specific purpose like a festival, others are less restricted. The operating rules are similar to those described by Fei (1943), some associations renew their membership at the end of a cycle and act on a semi-permanent basis. The article has information on default arrangements and mentions special pork societies, for the purchase of pork in bulk for the members for Chinese New Year.

Travancore. 1956. The Travancore Banking Enquiry Committee The Government of Travancore.
Cited by Sethi above.

Tschakert, H. 1976. Handwerkliche Genossenschaften und EKUB-Sparve-reine in Ethiopien. *Zeitshrift fur das gasamte Genossenschaftswesen* **28** (2). This article has some statistical data on the volume of savings in the 1963-73 period.

USAID 1973. *Spring Review of Small Farmer Credit* Washington D. C.: USAID.
These volumes contain papers on savings in the informal sector. Some appear in other publications.

van der Waal, K.& Sharp, J. 1988. The Informal Sector: A New Resource. *South African Keywords* (eds) E. Boonzaier & J. Sharp. Cape Town, David Philip, pp 136-152.

Velez-Ibanez, C. 1983. Social Diversity, Commercialization and Organizational Complexity of Urban Mexican/Chicano Rotating Credit Associations: Theoretical and Empirical Issues of Adaptation. *Human Organization* **41** (2), 107.
Not consulted.

Velez-Ibanez, C. G. 1985. *Bonds of Mutual Trust: The Cultural Systems of Rotating Credit Associations among Urban Mexicans and Chicanos*. New Brunswick, New Jersey: Rutgers University Press.

This is a study which looks at ROSCAs in Mexico and Mexican Americans in prison.

Wai, U. T. 1992. What Have We Learned about Informal Finance in Three Decades? In *Informal Finance in Low-Income Countries*. (eds) D. W. Adams & D. A. Fitchett. Boulder: Westview Press, pp 337-348.
Knowledge of and interest in the informal sector has increased greatly. The contribution of the sector is seen to be more positive and more significant. Moreover all classes are involved and the contacts between the informal and formal are more complex and numerous than formerly realised. There are a few paragraphs on ROSCAs.

Wainaina, N. 1989. *Indigenous Savings and Credit Schemes for Women in Kenya* SIDA.
The study was undertaken in 1989 in Kajiado, Kiambu, Kitui, Siaya, and Nairobi. It looks at ways in which agencies can build upon the traditions and existence of self-help groups among women. It considers the strengths and limitations of the associations. The membership, age, location and main activities of each group interviewed are given in table form. The author seems ignorant of ROSCAs in other parts of the world. (She mentions *susu* in Ghana.) Chapter 3 describes the case histories. Male support and encouragement were noted as key factors in leading to the groups' success in Kajiado. The author looks at the record of links with development agencies (pp. 62-3). There is a useful bibliography.

Warmington, W. A. 1958. Savings and Indebtedness among Cameroon's Plantation Workers. *Africa* **28** (4), 329-343.
Not consulted.

Warry, W. 1986. Kafaina: Female Wealth and Power in Chauve, Papua New Guinea. *Oceania* **57**, 4-21.
The article considers *woki meri* (savings and loans) movement. It does not appear to be rotating. The author agrees with Sexton's thesis that the *woki meri* is an organized collective response by women to the erosion of their economic status over the last 50 years. (*Kafaina* means shell or coin.)

Webb, N. 1989. *Informal Credit Markets in Cape Town, Guguletu: a Case Study*. University of Cape Town.
Not consulted.

Webb, P. 1988. *The Role of Irrigated Rice in Transforming Farm Household Relations in the Gambia*. The thesis considers (p.334) the role of formal credit made available by moneylenders and co-operatives in Georgetown, Gambia.

Williams, G. & Johnson, M. 1983. The *arisan* : a Tool for Economic Development ? *Prisma* **29**, 66-73.
This is an important work, based on first-hand fieldwork by the authors. They see the *arisan* as leading to a different type of savings and loan association. The work is cited in Hospes (1992). The authors believe that the type of *arisan* found in urban areas and popular among the elite owes much to the Chinese *hui* model. They paint a very different picture from Geertz who wrote of the drawing of lots to determine the order of receipt of funds; now there is a system of bidding.

Williamson, M. B. 1954. Rehabilitation and Development of Agriculture, Forestry and Fisheries in South Korea. FAO.
The report advised the Republic of Korea to encourage co-operative activity with special reference to the *ke* tradition.

Wilson, M., Mafeje, A. 1963. *Langa: A Study of Social Change in an African Township*. Cape Town: Oxford University Press.

The term *umgalelo* (pouring) club was common in Cape Town, but among the working class only. In Johannesburg there were middle class associations. The authors note the great variations of age and social class within a club, and the relatively small membership.

Wilsworth, M. 1979. Poverty and Survival: The Dynamics of Redistribution and Sharing in a Black South African Township. *Social Dynamics* 5 (1), 14-25.
Wilsworth describes the lending of money and the taking of interest in the *umgalelo*.

Wipper, A. 1984. Women's Voluntary Associations. In *African Women South of the Sahara* (eds) M. J. Hay & S. Strichter. London: Longman, pp 66-86.
This is not a very useful article. It does mention *nanamei akpee* in Ghana.

World Bank 1987. *Indonesia: Rural Credit Sector Review (vol. 1)*. World Bank.
Not consulted.

Wu, D. Y. 1974. To Kill Three Birds with One Stone. The Rotating Credit Associations of Papua New Guinea Chinese. *American Anthropologist* 1 (3), 565-584.
The author takes the same line as Kurtz that the associations are not a 'middle rung' but a response to deprivation. Background information on the community is drawn from the 1966 census. *Hui* are important for Chinese storekeepers, who are ashamed to borrow from moneylenders and do not have tangible assets to use as collateral. Default levels are low. Three types of *hui* exist (here the author draws on the work of Yang and Fei). *Lun hui* are described. The work is based on field trips 1971-73. The author writes that Ardener's inability to solve the problem of why ROSCAs exist in some societies and not in others is because the whole context — socio-political, cultural and economic as well as the structural features of the associations need to be taken into account.

Yang, L.-S. 1952. *Money and Credit in China. A Short History*. Cambridge, M. A.: Harvard University Press.
The book covers the various types of *hui*. *Lun hui* is the rotating credit association.

# INDEX TO CITATIONS

Note: Only the name of the first author is listed in cases of multi-authorship.

## AFRICA

**Cameroon**
Ardener, 1964; Bekolo-Ebe, 1987; Bouman, 1976; Brenner, 1989; Buysse, 1976; Chem-Langhee, 1988; deLancey, 1977; deLancey, 1978; deLancey, 1978; deLancey, 1987; Devereux, 1987; Dievot, n.d.; Haggblade, 1978; Harteveld, 1972; Illy, 1973; Jiggins, 1989; Meyer, 1940; Niger-Thomas, 1992; Rowlands, 1994; Seibel, 1985; Soen, 1971; Warmington, 1958

**Ethiopia**
Almedom, 1991, 1992, 1994; Altaye, 1991; Araya, 1984; Aredo, 1991; Asfaw, 1958; Baker, 1986; Begashaw, 1977; Begashaw, 1978; Chilke, 1983; Comhaire, 1966; Central Statistical Office, 1982; Gedamu, 1972; Levine, 1972; Lewis, 1988; Miracle, 1980; Padmanabhan, 1988; Pankhurst, 1958; Rahmato, 1991; Tschakert, 1976

**Gambia**
Ceesay-Marenah, 1982; Madge, 1991; Webb, 1988

**Ghana**
Adjetey, 1978; Ahulu, 1988; Aryeetey, 1990; Aryeetey, 1991; Bentil, 1988; Bortei-Doku, 1994; Gabianu, n. d.; Geertz, 1962; Holst, 1990; Holt, 1991; Little, 1962; Maison, 1988; Mendez, 1990; Newark, 1990; Nikoi, 1990; Robertson, 1982; Sanneh, 1975; Wainaina, 1989.

**Ivory Coast**
Lewis, 1976

**Kenya**
Burja, 1975; Due, 1990; Mendez, 1990; Nelson, 1992; von Pische, 1975; Wainaina, 1989

**Liberia**
Massing, 1974

**Nigeria**
Adeyemo, 1983; Adeyeye, 1970; Ardener, 1953; Barnes, 1975; Bascom, 1952; Bouman, 1979; Chilke, 1983; Ezeabasili, 1960; Firth, 1964; Ijere, 1963; Isong, 1958; Jerome, 1991; Katzin, 1964; Mbat, 1985; Mendez, 1990; Nadel, 1942; Nafziger, 1977; Ngozi, 1982; Nwabughuogu, 1984; Nwabughuogu, n.d.; Odozi, 1983; Okonjo, 1977; Okonjo, 1979; Okorie, 1976; Olodimu, 1984; Osuntogun, 1981; Ottenberg, 1959; Ottenberg, 1968; Owualah, 1984; Schildkrout, 1982; Seibel, 1992

**Rwanda**
Lacville 1991

**Sierre Leone**
Eldjik, 1992; Johnny, 1985; Little, 1962; Nwabughuogu, n.d.; Webb, 1988

**Somalia**
Summerfield, n.d.

**South Africa**
Burman, 1994; Coplan, 1979; Hellman, 1934; Hellman, 1935; Kokoali, 1987; Krige, 1934; Kuper, 1960; Lukhele, 1988; Lukhele, 1990; n.d., 1987; Phillips, n.d.; Ross, 1990; Thomas, 1989; Thomas, 1989; van der Waal, 1988; Webb, 1989; Wilson, 1963

**Tanzania**
Due, 1990; Massengo, 1992

**Uganda**
Bailey, 1990; Bailey, 1990; Heald, 1986; Miracle, 1980

**Zaire**
Cuevas, 1991; Miracle, 1980; Miracle, 1980b; Otero, 1989

**Zambia**
Due, 1982; Miracle 1980; Miracle, 1980b
**Zimbabwe**
Jiggins, 1985; Mendez, 1990

## ASIA

**China**
Fei, 1946; Gamble, 1944; Gamble, 1954; Geertz, 1962; Kulp, 1925; Lein-Sheng, 1952; Smith, 1899; Smith, 1982;Topley, 1964; Williams, 1983; Wu, 1974; Yang, 1952
**Hong Kong**
Topley, 1964
**India**
Ahooja-Patel, 1990; Anderson, 1966; Benedict, 1964; Berger, 1989; Bhende, 1986; Bouman, 1979; Bouman, 1989; Bouman, 1992; Burman, 1994; Chilke, 1983; Geertz, 1962; Ghose, 1943; Heyzer, 1990; Jain, 1929; Katzin, 1959; Kaur, 1990; Government of Kerala, 1972; Krishnan, 1959; Logan, 1887; Mayoux, 1994; Nash, 1964; Nayar, 1973; Nayar, 1986; Nayar, 1992; Rhadhakrishnan, 1975; Sethi, 1994; Shanmugan, 1989; Shanmugan, 1991; Srinivasan, 1994; Subbarama, 1925; Timberg, 1984; Wai, 1957
**Indonesia**
Berger, 1989; Biggs, 1991; Bouman, 1989; Bouman, 1992; Dewey, 1964; Geertz, 1962; Ghate, 1986; Hospes, 1992; Kern, 1986; Lindauer, 1971; Martin-Schiller, 1989; Mendez, 1990; Mubyarto, 1987; Pananek, 1988; Rustam, 1986; Scheepens, 1974; Seibel, 1992; Williams, 1983
**Japan**
Asakura, 1961; Campbell, 1962; Central Bank of Japan, 1961; Embree, 1939; Embree, 1946; Geertz, 1962; Hendry, 1981; Hendry, 1992; Ikeda, 1918; Ito, 1952; Izumida, 1992; Japan, 1961; Kawashima, 1944; Keigo, n.d.; Knez, n.d.; Kyokai, 1971; Smith, 1982; Tokutaro, 1962
**Korea**
Campbell, 1962; Donald, 1976; Knez, n.d.; Light, 1972; Light, 1988; Light, 1992; von Stockhausen, 1988; Williamson, 1954
**Malaysia**
Heyzer, 1990; Holst, 1990; Shanmugan, 1989; Shanmugan, 1991; Swift, 1964
**Mauritius**
Benedict, 1964
**Nepal**
Heyzer, 1990; Messerschnidt, 1972; Messerschnidt, 1973; Seibel, 1988; Seibel, 1992
**Papua New Guinea**
Burkins, 1984; Fernando, 1992; Heyzer, 1990; Sexton, 1982; Skeldon, 1980; Strathern, 1975; 1980; Wu, 1974
**Philippines**
Agabin, 1989; Lamberte, 1988; Lamberte, 1988; Lamberte, 1992b; Seibel, 1992
**Sri Lanka**
Bouman, 1984; Bouman, 1988; Fernando, 1986; Sanderatru, 1992
**Taiwan**
Donald, 1976; Ong, n.d.
**Thailand**
Chotigeat, 1985
**Tibet**
Messerschnidt, 1972
**Vietnam**
Barton, 1977; Bouman, 1979; Geertz, 1962

## AMERICAS

**Caribbean**

Ahooja-Patel, 1990; Besson, 1994; Bonnett, 1976; Bonnett, 1981; Crowley, 1953; Gomez, 1990; Herskovits, 1947; Katzin, 1959; Levin, 1975; Manhertz, 1979; Melville, 1947; Mendez, 1990; Miracle, 1971; Nash, 1964; Norville, 1969; Smith, 1964

**Latin America**
Adams, 1979; Adams, 1988; Ahooja-Patel, 1990; Berger, 1989; Chandavarkar, 1985; Christen, 1992; Cope, 1979; Fischer, 1988; Gomez, 1990; Hospes, 1988; Konig, 1990; Kurtz, 1973; Kurtz, 1978; Ladman, 1990; Mendez, 1990; Miracle, 1971; Nash, 1964; Otero, 1989; Velez-Ibanez, 1982; Velez-Ibanez, 1985

**United States of America**
Bonnett, 1976; Bonnett, 1981; Kurtz, 1973; Light, 1972; Light, 1988; Light, 1994; Symons, 1984; USAID, 1973

## EUROPE

**Cyprus**
Khatib-Chahidi, 1992
**England**
Almedom, 1992; Srinivasan, 1992; Summerfield, n.d.; Tebbut, 1983
**Turkey**
Adams, 1979; Koufopoulou, 1992

## WOMEN
Adams, 1988; Adjetey, 1978; Ahooja-Patel, 1990; Almedom, 1991; Almedom, 1994; Aredo, 1991; Aryeetey, 1991; Aziz, 1977; Bascom, 1952; Begashaw, 1978; Berger, 1989; Besson, 1994; Bortei-Doku, 1994; Bouman, 1976; Bouman, 1984; Bouman, 1992; Burja, 1975; Burman, 1994; Ceesay-Marenah, 1982; deLancey, 1978; deLancey, 1987; Due, 1982; Due, 1990; Due, 1991; Fernando, 1992; Geertz, 1962; Gomez, 1990; Hellman, 1934; Hendry, 1981; Hendry, 1992; Heyzer, 1990; Holt, 1991; Holt, 1991; Hospes, 1988; Hospes, 1992; Hospes, 1992b; Jellicoe, 1968; Jiggins, 1985; Jiggins, 1989; Kaur, 1990; Khatib-Chahidi, 1994; Kiernan, 1977; Knez, n.d.; Koufopoulou, 1994; Kuper, 1944; Lewis, 1976; Light, 1988; Light, 1992; Little, 1957; Little, 1962; Little, 1972; Little, 1973; Lukhele, 1990; Lycette, 1984; Madge, 1991; March, 1986; Massengo, 1992; Mayoux, 1992; Mbat, 1985; McKee, 1989; McKee, Mendez, 1990; Nelson, 1994; Nguyen, 1949; Niger-Thomas, 1994; Nikoi, 1990; Okeyo, 1979; Okonjo, 1977; Okonjo, 1979; Olivier, 1990; Osuntogun, 1981; Otero, 1989; Ottenberg, 1968; Pananek, 1988; Robertson, 1982; Ross, 1990; Rowlands, 1994; Schildkrout, 1982; Seibel, 1992; Sethi, 1994; Sexton, 1982b; Smith, 1982; Srinivasan, 1992; Summerfield, 1994; Szabo, 1992; Tebbut, 1983; Thomas, 1989; von Stockhausen, 1988; Wainaina, 1989.

www.ingramcontent.com/pod-product-compliance
Ingram Content Group UK Ltd.
Pitfield, Milton Keynes, MK11 3LW, UK
UKHW060343150426
5217IPUK00030B/2094